ANTHROPOLOGICAL PAPERS

MUSEUM OF ANTHROPOLOGY, UNIVERSITY OF MICHIGAN

No. 8

Essays on Archaeological Methods

Proceedings of a Conference Held under

Auspices of the Viking Fund

Edited by

JAMES B. GRIFFIN

ANN ARBOR

UNIVERSITY OF MICHIGAN PRESS, 1951

© 1951 by the Regents of the University of Michigan
The Museum of Anthropology
All rights reserved

ISBN (print): 978-1-949098-35-8
ISBN (ebook): 978-1-951519-59-9

Browse all of our books at
sites.lsa.umich.edu/archaeology-books.

Order our books from the University of Michigan
Press at www.press.umich.edu.

For permissions, questions, or manuscript queries,
contact Museum publications by email at umma-
pubs@umich.edu or visit the Museum website at
lsa.umich.edu/ummaa.

Contents

	Page
Introduction . . . . By James B. Griffin	1
Recent Advances in Surveying Techniques and Their Application to Archaeology . . . . By Albert C. Spaulding	2
The Use of Earth-moving Machinery in Archaeological Excavations . . . . By Waldo R. Wedel	17
Collaboration among Scientific Fields with Special Reference to Archaeology . . . . By Frederick Johnson	34
Recent Developments in the Treatment of Archaeological Textiles . . . . By Junius Bird	51
Principles in the Conservation of Mural Paintings . . . . By Rutherford J. Gettens	59
Chemical Analysis of Fossil Bone . . . . By Sherburne F. Cook	73
Metallurgical Analyses and Their Aid to Archaeology . . . . By William C. Root	85
Applications of X Ray to Archaeology . . . . By Paul F. Titterington	94
Carbon^{14} Dating . . . . By Donald Collier	97
Ceramic Technology as an Aid to Cultural Interpretation--Techniques and Problems . . . . By Frederick R. Matson	102

	Page
The Use of Mathematical Formulations in Archaeological Analysis By George W. Brainerd	117
The Use of IBM Machines in Analyzing Anthropological Data By Frederick P. Thieme	128
Final Session	133
Participants	143
Selected Bibliography	145

ESSAYS ON ARCHAEOLOGICAL METHODS

Introduction

James B. Griffin

During the meetings of the Twenty-ninth International Congress of Americanists, held in New York in September, 1949, conversations with various archaeologists indicated that a conference on archaeological field and laboratory techniques would serve as a stimulant in adopting information and adapting it to archaeological purposes. It was felt that a review of practices used by archaeologists in field and laboratory work, supplemented by papers read by associated technical experts, would afford an excellent opportunity for the exchange of ideas and problems. Publication of the papers and the pertinent discussions would then give wide dissemination to the current procedures and specialized techniques. It was hoped thereby to improve the general level of archaeological practices and, more important, to stimulate further research in the application of knowledge in other scientific fields to archaeological interpretation. With the enthusiastic support of the Viking Fund, Inc., of New York City (now the Wenner-Gren Foundation for Anthropological Research), it was possible to assemble a representative group in New York City in March, 1950. Publication of the proceedings has also been made possible by a grant from the Wenner-Gren Foundation.

Recent Advances in Surveying Techniques and Their Application to Archaeology

Albert C. Spaulding

After fairly extensive consultation with a number of archaeologists and a quick review of the published literature, I have decided that "recent" should be defined as any development after the time of Leonardo da Vinci. This situation is the result of the nature of the relationship of surveying to archaeology; it is not a commentary on the character of archaeologists, although it may be true that a distaste for mathematics has exercised a certain positive selective influence on the personnel of archaeology. However this may be, surveying is a drudging but indispensable chore which takes up time that might better be devoted to actual excavation and observation. An efficient field operation must accordingly adopt the simplest and fastest surveying techniques capable of producing the required accuracy in locating archaeological detail, just as it must adopt efficient methods of transportation. It is my opinion that the greatest possibility for generally increased efficiency lies in a better understanding of the fundamental operations of plane surveying, both in theory and as working techniques, so that an intelligent selection can be made to fit particular circumstances.

There are only two basic operations in planimetric surveying, measurement of horizontal distance and measurement of direction in the horizontal plane. It is also necessary in archaeological work to consider the vertical component, that is, to measure differences in elevation. These measurements may be made entirely on the ground, or they may be made on aerial or ground photographs with the aid of ground control. Surveying on the ground is the basic procedure and will be considered first.

The more important available techniques for measuring distances are the tape, stadia system, gradienter, and, possibly, the range finder. Of these, the tape is by far the most generally useful and accurate. I do not know of any recent advances in the design or construction of tapes. The stadia method is also well known and is exceedingly handy for plane table topography at medium and small scales. Its close relative is the gradienter (Stebbinger drum), which is a micrometer drum on the vertical motion of a transit or alidade. It is so adjusted as to elevate or depress the horizontal wire one foot on the rod for each 100 feet of distance with a full turn of the micrometer screw. The main advantage of the gradienter is that it can be used at longer distances than the orthodox wire intercept, but this ability is of dubious value for most archaeological work. The range finder, another item by no means new, may deserve serious consideration for some purposes, chiefly because it eliminates the services of a rodman. My own experience with the range finder is very limited, but the Coast and Geodetic Survey reports for a 30-centimeter instrument a probable error for a single reading of less than 1.5 per cent at 50-100 meters, less than 2 per cent at 100-250 meters, and less than 3 per cent at 250-500 meters. The probable error of the mean of six readings is substantially less. I do not know where, or whether, such instruments are available commercially, or how convenient they are under actual field conditions.

The relative directions of pointings can be measured on the horizontal graduated circle of a compass or transit, the immediate product being a pocketful of notes, or they can be recorded graphically by the plane table method. The plane table with telescopic alidade is, of course, the traditional equipment of the topographer and seems to be favored by a good many archaeologists. It has been my experience that the simple, open-sight alidade is superior to the telescopic type for large-scale mapping of features owing to the ease with which it can be pointed. A special type of direction-measuring instrument is the 90-degree prism, sometimes combined in one mounting with other types of prisms. The prism is an accurate and very compact device.

A number of operating procedures are possible through the use of various combinations of distance- and direction-measuring techniques. When field techniques of this variety are combined with a considerable number of plotting methods, the plans and sections which are the final product may be the result of dozens of different combinations. I should say at the outset that I do not know which of the many possibilities is the best; the choice is always contingent on such factors as the nature of the site, the budget of the excavating agency, the personal preferences of the excavator, and his estimate of significant accuracy.

The simplest technique for determining the horizontal

relationship of archaeological detail is that of the tie line survey. This sort of survey is made with the tape alone and is based on the fact that a triangle with three known sides can be plotted with a beam compass or dividers, or its angles can be computed and the results plotted in several different ways. It is well adapted to relatively flat areas, and a high order of accuracy is possible.

Perhaps the next simplest method, and one which has many desirable characteristics, is the plane table survey. The plane table outfit with telescopic alidade and magnetic needle can be used for every operation of surveying. The most effective way of using the plane table is to establish a few control stations by careful triangulation and to find the location of subsequent setups on the sheet and the proper orientation of the board by graphic 3-point resection. Plotting of points and delineation of contours or other features proceeds rapidly with the plane table method. The finished product is constructed in the field while the mapper still has the situation before him, with the result that blunders are noticeable and can be corrected promptly. Fewer shots are needed because of the mapper's ability to observe the situation directly and constantly. On the debit side, plane table work is quite dependent on good weather; its accuracy is absolutely limited by graphic errors in drawing rays and plotting points (this is a very weak objection for archaeological work); and the plane table is not easy to set over a point (this is the reason why 3-point resection is the traditional and recommended procedure) and consequently is not a good instrument for laying out excavation units or grid systems. I do not think that these objections are particularly grave ones.

The compass and transit can be considered together because of their fundamental similarity. By their use bearings or azimuth are measured on a graduated circle, and the results, combined with measured distances, are plotted with a protractor or by computing rectangular co-ordinates. The advantages of the compass are obvious; it is compact, inexpensive, and, if carefully handled, is capable of results sufficiently accurate for most archaeological purposes. Some compasses (notably the Brunton type) are equipped with bubbles so that levels can be read, and the result is a complete surveying instrument. Compass surveys, however, are not capable of providing anything like the precision attainable with the transit or plane table, chiefly because of unpredictable magnetic variations, absence of a vernier index, and a short base line of sight. The transit in its complete form (with compass, level bubble, and vertical circle) is a universal surveying instrument. It can be used efficiently for triangulation, traverse, and radiation and is unquestionably the best instrument for laying out a predetermined control system such as the rectangular grid. It has an important general advantage over the plane table method in that the measurements can be reduced to rectangular co-ordinates for plotting entirely by computing methods without any intermediate graphic steps to weaken the final solution. This advantage is lost if the transit pointings are plotted with a simple protractor. The point of origin and azimuths of transit cuts can also be established by 3-point resection, either by computation or by graphic methods. The transit also has disadvantages. In the first place, some archaeologists simply do not like transits—they are dismayed by the array of bubbles, thumbscrews, and verniers. One well-established field man protested that he had never succeeded in leveling a transit. In the second place, most archaeologists object to computations and, in fact, refuse emphatically to have anything to do with trigonometric functions and logarithms. The result is that transit notes are often plotted with a small protractor, a method better suited to compass bearings. Another objection is that blunders in reading or recording are not apparent until the notes have been plotted, when there may be no possibility of checking. Although a little practice will overcome some of these difficulties, it seems doubtful that the transit will ever achieve any great popularity in archaeological circles for anything but establishing grid systems and leveling.

The rectangular grid system itself should be the subject of some discussion. It is very extensively used in the United States, perhaps more extensively than its intrinsic merits warrant. Its appeal seems to lie in the fact that it is easily plotted on a site map (already prepared co-ordinate paper is often used), that it provides so many control points that any specific detail point can be located quickly, that individual squares can be described by a simple verbal formula, and that the squares, or combinations of them, are convenient excavation units of comparable size. It is, moreover, comparatively easy to establish on the ground. Some of these advantages are more apparent than real, and the field man might well consider alternatives. The essential features of a control system are a point of origin and a defined direction; any additional features must be justified on a basis of convenience, not of necessity. In a number of instances elaborate grids have been established and marked by a forest of stakes at 5-foot intersections, with perhaps no more than a fifth of the stakes actually used in plotting detail. Aside from the wasted effort, one is always tripping over the stakes. A more rational approach would be to establish a few intersections at 100-foot intervals (or whatever lengths the longest tape available can measure), and to mark other intersections as needed with chaining pins. A still more rational approach in some situations would be to establish by triangulation or closed traverse four or five control points, place the excavations wherever the best archaeological judgment dictates, and then find out where the excavations are by plane table, compass, or transit resection, intersection, or any other method. Detail within excavation units can be plotted with the aid of a small unit grid system or on a large-scale plane table sheet.

Measurement of differences in elevation can be accomplished by direct leveling with a bubble vial attached to a straightedge or chalk line, a telescope, or some other type of sight line (particularly the hand level or Brunton compass). This sort of leveling is well understood and requires no lengthy comment. I am inclined to think that the hand level is a neglected instrument—it is cheap, compact, easy to adjust, and will yield better results than would be thought possible from a casual inspection. The Chicago rod is a device not too well known, but useful when many readings are to be taken from one setup. It has an adjustable foot and movable tags for the footmarks. The rod can be adjusted to give the true elevation as a direct rod reading, thus eliminating the usual subtraction of the rod reading from the elevation of the instrument. Special types of surveyor's levels will not be considered, since the bubbles attached to telescopic alidades and transits are more than adequate for any type of archaeological work. The type of telescopic instrument called a "builder's level" deserves serious consideration for the limited budget. It is typically a small Wye level of fair quality with a horizontal circle and 5-minute vernier. It is much lower in price than the standard instruments and much better in quality than the mail order "farm transits." A second method of measuring differences of elevation is indirect, or trigonometric, leveling. This is accomplished by measuring vertical angles to points of known distance (either slope or horizontal distance) and computing the difference of elevation by tangent or sine formula. This method is characteristic of topographic work, in which great accuracy is of no importance and the saving in the number of setups required is very important. It is usually employed in conjunction with stadia or gradienter distance readings, either by means of a special arc (the Beaman arc) graduated so as to give direct readings of factors which yield true horizontal distances and differences of elevation when multiplied by the stadia intercept, or by reading the vertical angle and obtaining the difference of elevation with stadia tables or with a special stadia slide rule. The slide rule is faster and more accurate than the Beaman arc, but it is one more piece of equipment to carry. This sort of leveling, especially the Beaman arc method, is most commonly used by the plane table topographer, but it is equally suitable for the transit. Its most important use in archaeology is in making topographic maps of large sites having considerable relief.

I have no comment on the question of the absolute accuracy required in archaeological surveying. This is entirely a matter of the judgment of the excavator, and there is no rigid criterion to fit every situation. From the standpoint of the surveyor all that can be said is that the methods used should be consistent, since the final plotting of a point is no better than the weakest step in determining its position. Control systems should be somewhat stronger than the desired final result; for example, if elevations to the nearest tenth of a foot are required, the elevations of the benchmarks from which the final readings are made should be measured to the nearest hundredth of a foot. On the other hand, determination of benchmark elevations to the nearest thousandth of a foot would be an absurd refinement. In contour mapping in most situations any attempt to determine spot elevations more closely than a tenth of the contour interval is wasted effort. These principles apply equally, of course, to determinations of horizontal position. There is no conceivable advantage in using, say, 5-place tables of trigonometric functions to work up compass bearings, or in worrying about the eccentric effect of the alidade blade on pointings when the distances are measured by the stadia method. Apart from the question of internal consistency, errors of closure are the best gauge of the general usefulness of a given technique.

If these errors are consistently much smaller than the estimated significant error, the system is overly precise and a time waster.

Surveying from photographs is a comparatively new field which has many archaeological applications. The usefulness of the vertical aerial photographs so widely available in the United States in the archaeological survey is too well known to require discussion. It is perhaps not so generally known that identified points on the photographic print can be transferred to the standard map conveniently and quite accurately, thus taking care of the problem of the position and orientation of sites. The process is a simple one of identifying several common points on map and photograph and then transferring the desired photographic points to the map by a simple proportional adjustment. If overlapping photographs are available, a still more precise radial line plotting method can be used. When sufficient ground control is available and the photographs are of suitable scale, planimetric and topographic maps of sites can be prepared directly from the photographs, often at a great saving in expensive field time. Oblique aerial photographs can also be used for mapping, although the process is more laborious.

Mapping from ground vertical and oblique photographs is a promising field as yet little explored by archaeologists. Merrill has reported successful use of vertical photographs at Coclè, and Coe has developed a similar system which is very impressive in my opinion. Coe's method was designed for relatively flat North Carolina village sites with innumerable features (pits, postholes, and so forth) just below the plow line. An ordinary 4-by 5-inch press camera and a rather heavy tripod some 10 to 12 feet high were the basic equipment items. After the plowed earth was cleared off, the camera was mounted on the tripod and centered on a 5-foot unit of the site grid system. The stakes marking the grid appeared on the ground glass and were scaled to make sure that the optical axis of the camera was normal to the plane of the cleared square (in theory only three corners can be held, but this objection had no practical significance). A small label identifying the square was placed on the ground and appeared on the negative. Finally, projection prints to a fixed scale were made, great care being used to match adjoining prints in tone. The prints were trimmed and laid in controlled mosaics of standard size, say 100 by 50 feet ground measure. The result was superb from the standpoint of interpretation and mapping. Tracings of features made from the mosaic showed more detail, and showed it more accurately, than did the maps prepared on the spot by conventional methods. It must be admitted, however, that the skillful and tedious darkroom work necessary is a disadvantage. I can think of no major improvements on the system. Minor improvements might include better targets than stakes to mark grid intersections, use of topographic film to avoid negative distortion, and possibly other small advances.

The use of horizontal and oblique ground photographs for mapping will probably increase in the future. Their utility rests on the fact that it is possible to draw or compute true vertical and horizontal angles when the position and elevation of three ground points identifiable on the photograph are known. This general statement is of remarkably little interest to archaeologists because the solution requires dealing with simultaneous linear equations and, to be really elegant, with least squares adjustments. But if the position of the camera station is obtained in advance, if the focal length of the camera is known, if a true azimuth to at least one photo point is measured, and if a pair of targets defining a level line is set, mapping can proceed at once from the print by simple graphical methods with ordinary drafting instruments. If more elaborate plotting instruments of the type of the photoalidade or phototransit are available, vertical and horizontal angles can be read directly, precisely as if the observer had the ground in front of him instead of a photograph. A field party equipped with a camera alidade (an alidade fitted with a surveying camera in addition to the telescope) or a camera transit could obtain adequate data for complete surveys of large sites in a fraction of the time necessary for orthodox ground mapping techniques. A valuable supplementary item for such a party would be a Land camera to produce prints for point identification and annotation at the time that the camera was occupied. This sort of survey would be particularly well adapted to remote areas where field time is at a premium and complex mapping problems exist. It is probably well to point out, however, that photogrammetrical techniques are unfortunately not magical. They do not eliminate ground surveying; in general, it is only possible to measure angles on photographs, distances being obtained by intersection techniques; certain troublesome details, such as negative and print distortion, must be overcome.

In regard to really new developments, I have little to say. The chief item which comes to mind is radar, which is sheer magic so far as I am concerned. It undoubtedly has great possibilities as a mapping device, and archaeologists should adopt a policy of watchful waiting.

DISCUSSION

BRAINERD: The photomapper, developed in the Navy during the war, was designed with versatility and portability especially in mind. It weighs about sixty pounds and fits a suitcase-size case. It can be used to draw projections from any type of photograph available and will produce perspectives from plans or elevations. It can also be used like a camera lucida in copying, enlarging, and reducing drawings, in drawing from objects or photographs, in transferring information between maps drawn to different projections, and so forth. A good understanding of descriptive geometry is sufficient as a starting point in the operation of the instrument. An instruction manual is available.

In archaeology this instrument should be serviceable in working up maps and illustrations from field notes and photographs, both ground and aerial. There are many situations in which it is easier to take photographs than to make measured maps and drawings. In presentation of results perspective reconstructions often help. By this instrument they can be made rapidly from plans and elevations. It also may possibly be of use to physical anthropologists in mapping facial and body contours from photographs.

Inquiries may be made of the Office of Naval Research as to the availability of this instrument. It is possible that one may be obtained on loan for use in scientific experimentation.

GRIFFIN: I should like to ask how much instruction in surveying is given in a regular university course leading to a Ph. D. degree. Is it presumed that the student will pick up surveying in the field work which he does in various field schools or with a field party? How much instruction in surveying should an archaeologist have? Is he the one who is expected to know everything there is to know, or can he be allowed to hire someone to do this surveying work for him?

BREW: Jimmy as usual asks six questions at a time. The best way, I think, is for the student to pick up surveying on the job, working with someone he knows. This may be the case in some places. Plane tabling is very, very important to geologists. In the geology department at the University (Harvard), every spring vacation students go out and make a plane table map of Fresh Pond in Cambridge. Students in the anthropology department may enroll in the course as well as those in geology. In regard to hiring someone to do the surveying, it seems to me that depends on the size of the job. If you've got a small job you can do it yourself. If you've got a big job, you've got to hire somebody, because it's a full-time job on a big site. At the Awatovi excavations, carried on for five years in northeastern Arizona, we had a full-time surveyor all the time, who usually had a full-time or part-time assistant.

SPAULDING: That's another reason why it's important to choose the most economical method.

BREW: It depends on the man you have. I had an engineer once who refused to use a plane table because he said it wasn't accurate. I argued with him periodically all through the season, but he used a transit for everything. At the end of the season, he said he'd like to try the plane table — and he converted himself in ten minutes. Of course, at least ten to fifteen years ago in this country engineers thought that the plane table was a bad thing because it wasn't completely accurate.

I should like to point out that if we were engaged in building a bridge to carry trains with hundreds of human lives dependent upon the structure, a very high degree of surveying accuracy would be needed and justifiable. Such is not the case when an archaeological site is being mapped. A plane table is certainly accurate enough for our purposes.

The job is often too complex for simpler methods, however. For instance, when you get big mounds on those pueblo sites where there is 400 years' accumulation of masonry at all sorts of angles, sometimes a wall is just built on as a site builds up. A new type of masonry is built on top of the old wall, and you get a single column fifty feet high representing, from top to bottom, various types of masonry of different periods. In addition to that, someone will have changed the shape or even the orientation of a room as the structure grew, and you get quite a mix-up. In fact, the top map man at such a complex site is going to need a helper. At times we've had two men, not counting rodmen, working at once.

SPAULDING: Tangled situations of that sort can only be mapped accurately with a plane table.

BREW: I'm glad you mentioned the peep-sight alidade, because for individual work that's the best thing. In your case, that's standard equipment. In Europe, an archaeologist personally owns an open-sight alidade and a small plane table. Of course, you've got to tape the distances.

SPAULDING: That's all right for large-scale work. I'd like to say that as a result of having talked to a good many archaeologists in the past two years, I feel that there's a striving for too much accuracy. Everyone ought to ask himself why he's fussing around trying to get a one-one hundredth closure on a hundred-foot square. If you're talking about precise leveling and that sort of thing, there's no place for it in archaeology.

FORD: I've always found it most convenient to put in a fairly accurate grid and replace stakes as the excavations are carried down. That is done with a transit, not to pinpoint accuracy, but to one-one hundredth of a foot on the one hundred-foot corners. And instead of setting up a plane table and carefully drawing in a wall with alidade sights, it can be done quite simply by tape measurements from near-by stakes.

SPAULDING: I'm not arguing against grid systems as such, I'm just suggesting that we examine the situation carefully to see whether it's worth while to put in a grid.

FORD: There is also the matter of the size of the grid. Some people often make their grid units too small.

SPAULDING: Yes, they do, and they install a lot of control for which there'll be no conceivable use. There's an automatic tendency to think that the grid system is the right way to do it, that you're simply not doing archaeology if you don't have a forest of five-foot stakes extending over the site. This is not true. As a matter of fact, Jim, this method you mentioned is perfectly all right. In those circumstances, I would rather make a series of large-scale plane table sheets, which give the same results.

FORD: It's a matter of preference and convenience.

SPAULDING: That's right.

JOHNSON: You said that the plane table is sometimes difficult to use in certain climates?

SPAULDING: That's right. It does have the factor of being dependent on good weather with ordinary paper. But you can get what topographers call metal mount, which is an aluminum sheet with paper glued on both sides with the grain of the paper at right angles; that is, the grain of the paper is horizontal on one side of the sheet and vertical on the other side. These sheets are virtually tornado, wind-storm, fire, and theft proof. The Coast and Geodetic Survey reported that one of their men dropped a boat sheet on a metal mount in thirty feet of water. He retrieved it by putting a nail on the end of a plummet, stabbing the sheet through, and bringing it up. After they dried it off, the scale remained practically unchanged. There are also a number of plastic sheets which can be used in the rain.

JOHNSON: Also, you can build a shelter over the plane table. One of those old-fashioned umbrella stands could be used. Are those metal sheets with the paper available?

SPAULDING: They are generally made to order for the user. They're quite expensive, but both sides may be used.

RITCHIE: Has anyone but Coe attempted this mapping by photographing and putting together the prints of the site?

SPAULDING: I presume others have; I don't know. I'm familiar with Coe's method and it's a good enough example for this discussion.

RITCHIE: What do you do with a large site?

SPAULDING: Take a lot of photographs.

RITCHIE: Yes, I know, but do you cut the assembled map apart and then put it on a linen back so that you can fold it up? This big site map would cover the wall of a room larger than this one. How do you handle it?

SPAULDING: What you do is put it up in subunits, then file it in a big book with an index, so that you know what joins what.

RITCHIE: We've done something similar with burials, photographing each grave as found, cutting out the area around the burial, and pasting these sections together in the proper positions, then finally inking in the areas between the burials to provide a very realistic and striking picture of the orientation and relationship of the individual graves.

SPAULDING: Yes, I'm sure a number of people have used the method in one form or another.

RITCHIE: I never thought of doing it with the entire site.

SPAULDING: It's quite amazing. I compared the mosaics themselves with the map made on the ground by ordinary methods. The photographs showed everything mapped by ordinary methods and a good deal that wasn't.

RITCHIE: And by taking photographs at different levels or stages of the excavation a series of maps recording graphically the various components or succession of superimposed features at a site could be obtained.

ORCHARD: Have you any comment on the use of balloons for aerial mapping? The Oriental Institute uses them a good deal.

SPAULDING: No, I don't have any particular comment. It's obvious that in the absence of proper aerial mapping equipment substitutes could be devised to furnish photos for interpretation and perhaps for mapping. You have mentioned balloons, and somebody has used kites. In general, just any method may be used by which you can get a camera into the air.

RITCHIE: Wouldn't a helicopter be ideal because it is capable of being flown at a slow speed and very low elevation?

SPAULDING: Yes, it would, if you happened to have one around.

RITCHIE: Perhaps it might be possible to hire one.

WEDEL: Then, of course, there are standard types of planes.

SPAULDING: Yes, one of the small two-seater planes sold for sport would serve very well.

RITCHIE: Except that you'd be higher than you would be in a helicopter, and going faster.

SPAULDING: Yes. Still, you might be able to go down one hundred feet or so, correlating the speed of the camera with the speed of the plane. Of course, you have to have some means of pointing straight down if you want to take vertical photographs.

RITCHIE: Helicopters can hover over a spot.

JOHNSON: Does anyone know about the vibration of a helicopter, and whether that would make any difference?

SPAULDING: I shouldn't think it would make any difference. I have no idea how much a helicopter vibrates.

WEDEL: I recall a remark by Stirling that the vibration is rather high. I don't know how much photography he actually tried from a helicopter.

POLLOCK: How are oblique photographs rectified? Is it a practical procedure for archaeologists?

SPAULDING: It is, with the proper sort of equipment. Perhaps Mr. Brainerd's universal sketchmaster might be the answer. Oblique photographs can be used without rectification, but that's a tedious process. I wouldn't recommend rectification at all; rather, simply use the photograph as is. There are drafting table methods, and there are a number of exceedingly convenient machines, fascinating machines in fact, which have an easel on which the oblique photograph is mounted at the proper angle of depression or elevation. One machine has a little short-focus telescope, a remarkable thing with cross wires on it, the position of which corresponds to the focal length of the camera, so that you restore the perspective situation. The telescope is combined with an alidade blade and you just sit at a table, precisely as though you were doing plane table work through a window. These machines cost about $350, but it would be worth while if you had a complex mapping problem in some area where your field time is very expensive.

BRAINERD: In regard to this small instrument I spoke of, I believe that in a pueblo ruin if you had obliques to cover the area taken from a height of about thirty to forty feet, or even twenty feet, from a tree off the edge, and also if you took a series of floor levels of the site, you could get a complete set of plans and elevations.

SPAULDING: I'm sure a great deal of future work will be done along those lines.

BRAINERD: That's right. There are all sorts of combinations. If you have a plan and don't have the levels, you can superimpose an oblique photograph and get the altitudes from the photographs and work those out on the plan.

SPAULDING: In general, three good well-distributed points would provide sufficient content to enable use of the photograph for mapping.

ROUSE: I think perhaps we had better get on. We will now have to change our perspectives somewhat. We've been dealing with extremely accurate work. The next paper will be on something not so accurate.

WEDEL: I want to say at the outset that I'm not here on the defensive or to apologize for advocating the use of power machinery. It's my feeling as I look over this paper that it is really nothing more than a polysyllabic statement of the obvious.

The Use of Earth-Moving Machinery in Archaeological Excavations

Waldo R. Wedel

In the summer of 1946, when the Missouri River Basin Survey was just getting on its feet, one of my first endeavors on behalf of the project was an attempt to interest the Omaha district engineer, Missouri River Division, Corps of Engineers, in our archaeological salvage problem. As I waited in his outer office, I struck up a conversation with the executive officer, who had once been stationed at Fort Huachuca, Arizona, and while there had developed some casual interest in archaeological collecting. After I had regaled this gentlemen with an account of the nature and magnitude of the problems posed by the engineers' water-control program on the Missouri River in the Dakotas, he suggested pointedly: "You fellows better throw away your picks and shovels and learn to run bulldozers." Then came a brief but vivid recounting of the amount of material a bulldozer can remove per hour, followed by a rough calculation of how much time would be required to "clean up" a site covering a specified number of acres and lying at a given depth below ground. All this seemed to me an auspicious start, but unfortunately higher echelon was not equally sympathetic. As it turned out, nearly two years elapsed before systematic excavation by bulldozers was actually begun by the Missouri River Basin Survey, and then it came about first through the interest of the Bureau of Reclamation.

The idea of utilizing earth-moving power equipment, specifically bulldozers, road patrols, and similar heavy units, had already occurred, of course, to those of us charged with responsibility for the pending salvage program. Elsewhere, overburden removal by team and scraper or with power-driven devices has been tried, successfully and otherwise, more than once in American archaeology. In the Missouri Basin, paleontologists had availed themselves of the advantages of the bulldozers over hand tools where deeply buried materials were to be worked out. So far as we were aware, however, no one had yet undertaken the all-out excavation of a village site covering several acres and including house sites, cache pits, possibly graves, and other features as a planned mechanized project. The large-scale work carried out during CWA and WPA days was, in the very nature of things, based on the employment of large numbers of men and not on the systematic and sustained use of earth-moving machinery.

Several considerations gave impetus to our desire to include use of power equipment in the salvage program. In the first place, many of the foreseeable projects were coming up in regions of exceedingly limited manpower; the competition with construction companies striving to get what labor was available meant that wages were being bid upward beyond the limited resources of the River Basin Surveys. With unskilled labor drawing from 85 cents to $1.25 per hour, the funds allocated for archaeological salvage did not permit the assembling of large crews comparable to those of relief days. Yet the need for large-scale operations was, if anything, even greater than during the thirties, for we were working against a deadline that was already uncomfortably close—completion within perhaps six to ten years of more than 100 dams and major water-control projects of various kinds and the consequent obliteration of hundreds of archaeological sites. Faced thus with early deadlines and serious labor shortages plus limited allotments of money and of trained personnel, it seemed obvious that something more than shovels, whisk brooms, and enthusiasm would be needed for the job ahead.

Our chance came after the devastating flood of June 22, 1947, on Medicine Creek, in south-central Nebraska. Heavy property damage and loss of thirteen lives speedily raised the proposed Medicine Creek dam project from a very low construction priority to top place. Previously, reconnaissance by field parties of the River Basin Surveys and other agencies had disclosed a number of promising prehistoric sites on and near the proposed dam axis, as well as in the near-by borrow and work areas, and it now became apparent that these faced early obliteration. Through the good offices of the National Park Service, with whom the Smithsonian Institution already had a written understanding, a working agreement was reached between the Bureau of Reclamation, as the construction agency, and the River Basin Surveys. Under this agreement the Bureau furnished earth-moving machinery, a labor force varying from fifteen to twenty men, and labor supervision; the River Basin Surveys provided trained and experienced archaeologists who were responsible for planning and directing the scientific aspects of the work. On this basis comprehensive excavations were carried on from March 28 until August 20, 1948. Six village sites attributable to the Upper Republican horizon were more or less completely worked out, depending on the extent to which they would be affected by reservoir construction, and two small Woodland sites were also cleared. Full use was made at all times of all hand labor available, as well as of whatever earth-moving equipment was at the disposal of the archaeologists.

Power equipment has since been utilized for archaeological work by the River Basin Surveys on two other high-priority projects in the Missouri Basin. During November, 1948, a River Basin Surveys party excavated a small prehistoric burial mound situated on the spillway line of Fort Randall Dam, a Corps of Engineers project on the Missouri River south of Lake Andes, South Dakota. Again, during the summer of 1949, in the course of intensive surveys and excavations at Angostura Reservoir on the Cheyenne River south of Hot Springs, South Dakota, bulldozers were utilized from time to time in removing overburden at a number of nonpottery sites situated near the dam. Similar use of a bulldozer was also made by the University of Nebraska State Museum during 1948-49 in excavation of deeply buried prepottery sites at Medicine Creek Reservoir, Nebraska. These several projects gave a welcome variety to the conditions under which earth-moving equipment was given its first real test in archaeological excavation in the Missouri River Basin.

The sites excavated in the Medicine Creek area, like most others in the region which have not been subjected to long cultivation and excessive erosion, were overlaid by a sterile wind-deposited soil varying in thickness from six to nearly twenty inches. Beneath this was the old habitation level—a dark gray artifact- and refuse-bearing soil zone from six to twenty inches thick. Where the overlying dust mantle had not been broken by tillage or erosion, it supported a tight sod of buffalo grass; its surface was characteristically devoid of artifacts or other aboriginal traces, which were to be found along the broken edges of the terraces where the old occupational zone cropped out. In and below this buried occupational zone or "fossil" soil, of course, were to be found virtually all of the house sites, cache pits, midden deposits, and other archaeological features.

The earth-moving power equipment employed in this work consisted of a road patrol with ten-foot blade and, alternatively, a small bulldozer. The initial operations consisted of the stripping by bulldozer of a large sod-covered area known, or else suspected through previous testing with hand tools, to be underlaid with materials of archaeological interest. All elevations and other promising spots were denuded of sod and sterile overburden, and narrow exploratory trenches of varying width, depth, and length were cut in all directions across the presumed village site area. Where this stripping disclosed admixture of ashes, charcoal, mussel shells, and so forth, or revealed other evidences of features of possible archaeological significance, the road patrol was then brought into play. This instrument, with its longer blade, wider sweep, and more uniform depth and evenness of cut, removed another three to six inches of soil, usually to the point where the old habitation level itself lay exposed. Trained observers armed with shovels and trowels followed closely behind the road patrol to test freshly uncovered concentrations of refuse, burnt earth, ash, and similar extraneous materials. Where these tests disclosed a continuing admixture under the freshly bared surface, the immediate area was then staked out in ten-foot squares and uncovered with the usual hand tools—shovels, picks, trowels, and smaller implements, as needed. As this final operation got under way, the power machinery was used for removal from time to time of accumulating backdirt from the scene of immediate activity and for further exploratory work elsewhere in search of other archaeological features.

As work progressed on the larger village sites at Medicine Creek, interesting and hitherto unknown or obscure details about the native settlement patterns emerged. Once an area of two to eight acres had been completely stripped, it became apparent that the villages were laid out in markedly different fashion from those of the later historic period. Here and there on the cleared surfaces were visible spots of mixed soil from ten to twenty yards across; between them the soil appeared relatively clean and undisturbed. Further investigation with hand tools showed that the house sites occurred in small groups of two to four units each, with entrance passages opening toward the east, south, or southwest. In front of, or around, each doorway there was characteristically a small midden area, usually containing far more cultural debris than did the near-by house floor. Thus, when a well-marked midden area was exposed in the stripping, it became a relatively simple matter to find the associated house site a few feet to the north or west. Furthermore, it was found that most of the houses had been dug originally but little, if any, below the contemporary ground surface. Thus, there were usually no sharply defined wall lines to delimit the original structure, and its edges could be determined only from the disappearance of admixture in the soil as work was carried outward beyond the outer row of wall postholes.

The scattered clustering of house units in Upper Republican village sites, as contrasted with the compact arrangement in historic villages in the eastern plains, had been suspected before the large-scale operations at Medicine Creek. There remained, however, the disquieting thought that the earlier excavations may have uncovered only the more obvious house remains, and that between the structures so disclosed there might be much additional buried material. It now appears certain that scattered clusters of houses were the characteristic settlement pattern in Upper Republican days, and that the areas between house clusters were probably not contemporaneously inhabited or otherwise utilized in a manner that would leave archaeological traces.

There is, of course, nothing new or unique in the work done by the power machinery, as above described. It represents simply a device for rapid exploring and clearing of sterile deposits on an archaeological zone and for speedy and easy removal of useless backdirt. In meeting these two primary problems it does for the field archaeologist essentially what it does for the contractor or builder—it moves a great mass of sterile matrix at relatively small cost of time and human effort. In the course of a single afternoon, the road patrol in ground that has been tilled can sweep one to several acres crumb free before the stripped area dries out and again hides the newly exposed traces of aboriginal disturbance. In an area where house sites and other features are scattered and often lie many yards or even rods apart, no other method even approaches such a mechanical procedure for speed and effectiveness.

The mechanized operations employed at Medicine Creek in 1948 resulted, as I have already suggested, in the accumulation of a very considerable body of data regarding many aspects of the prehistoric occupancy of the locality. Among the outstanding contributions, it seems to me, is the evidence regarding the nature of the aboriginal settlement patterns and their implications for culture history in the region. It has long been suspected that the Woodland peoples lived in small groups on relatively obscure sites; the nature of their habitations and the exact character of their subsistence economy have remained obscure. The evidence from Medicine Creek in conjunction with that gathered in WPA days in central Nebraska indicates that the settlements were indeed small, with communities characteristically consisting apparently of not more than two or three house units, and that subsistence was probably based on hunting and gathering rather than on horticulture. For the later Upper Republican occupancy, the Medicine Creek data convincingly establish a settlement pattern of small scattered clusters of subrectangular earth lodges, situated with no apparent regard for defensive considerations and without defensive works. This archaeological evidence, based at Medicine Creek on the stripping of whole village sites, is in striking contrast to the later community patterns of the Plains village tribes. At the dawn of the historic period, the Pawnees and their contemporaries on the upper Missouri were residing in large communities probably numbering hundreds and even thousands of individuals, with houses built close together and surrounded by stockades or earthen defensive walls. It is true, of course, that this general trend had been suspected from previous smaller-scale work; but the large-scale operations at Medicine Creek have given us a much firmer foundation than was heretofore available from which to carry forward our interpretations. For thus providing within the short space of twenty-one weeks data that would otherwise have required several seasons of laborious digging on the part of many men with shovels, the power machinery was indispensable.

At Angostura and Fort Randall the archaeological conditions encountered were somewhat different from those at Medicine Creek. Many of the sites at Angostura were similarly buried under varying depths of wind-blown or other deposits. Cultural materials were much scarcer, however, and features consisted largely of various types of rock-filled or rock-lined hearths, roasting pits, and ash lenses scattered here and there on the erstwhile soil surfaces. Here the primary need was for large-scale stripping of overburden and largely sterile upper layers, and for long exploratory trenches to locate buried materials not apparent on the terrace surface.

Many hundreds of man hours were saved by a few hours' work with the bulldozer, and the results were far more satisfactory than they otherwise would have been.

At Fort Randall the problem was the salvage of scientific information from a burial mound facing early removal because of spillway construction. Under constant supervision of experienced field men, a Corps of Engineers bulldozer carefully sliced into the mound fill, beginning well away from one edge and working toward the center. Continuing checks of the fill were made with hand tools, and as burials, cultural materials, or other inclusions were encountered, these, too, were carefully scrutinized, recorded, and removed by hand. Within the space of a few hours' working time, the bulldozer cleared away culturally sterile soil that would have required many days of work on the part of men equipped only with shovels. It is probably true that this procedure resulted in fewer profile drawings of mound structure, at any rate in the direction transverse to the cuts made by the machine. Since there was ample evidence of the artificial character of the mound fill, and since its whole structure could be adequately studied or plotted throughout its entire extent at any stage of the operations, I doubt that the absence of a few transverse profiles constitutes a serious loss to science or that it will badly warp the conclusions derived from the work.

It may be worth pointing out that the bulldozer and the road patrol supplement each other rather well for work such as that done in 1948 at Medicine Creek. The bulldozer is the better tool where tough buffalo-grass sod must be broken through, where there is a considerable depth of sterile overburden the removal of which is a purely routine procedure that otherwise would involve the use of many men, shovels, and perhaps explosives, and where the spoil dirt represents a major problem because it must be concentrated in a relatively limited area and perhaps replaced at the close of operations. Properly handled and under certain soil conditions, it can also be very useful in the cutting of long profile trenches from which more precise excavation procedures can be profitably planned and carried on. The road patrol, on the other hand, is of greater usefulness in the rapid stripping of large areas where sod removal is not a problem and in providing a smooth dirt-free surface on which, so long as the soil remains relatively moist and fresh, evidence of man-made disturbance may be readily recognized.

With either bulldozer or road patrol a highly important item is the skill and know-how of the operator. He must have a clear understanding of exactly what he is to do. Moreover, he must be thoroughly familiar with the capabilities and limitations of his machine; if he overestimates its power or underestimates the particular cutting job at hand, he may be forced to back off for another try and thereby churn up the surface from which the archaeologist will be seeking his clues. With power machinery no less than with hand tools, a clean, fresh working face is of primary importance. An operator who, in addition to possessing mechanical skill and good judgment, can be indoctrinated with an interest in the particular problem at hand will often detect soil differences and extraneous materials almost as soon as his blade uncovers them. A prompt call at this stage for an experienced archaeologist with shovel and trowel may very materially expedite the operations.

Like any other technique in the field or laboratory, the use of earth-moving machinery on a large scale requires a certain minimum of forethought and planning. Unless the site under investigation is situated on a terrace or other elevation over whose sheer sides the backdirt can be gotten rid of once and for all, the excavation plans should include provision for the disposal of spoil dirt in certain readily accessible dump areas. With the bulldozer these dumps can be concentrated and built up to a considerable height, which facilitates return of the dirt to the work area if the property owner so wishes. With the road patrol, on the other hand, a much larger dump area is needed since the machine cannot maneuver, as the bulldozer, on its own tailings.

With regard to excavation procedure, it appears advisable that trenches and other cuts be pushed forward wherever possible on a broad even front so as not to obstruct the path of the machine with standing walls, pit edges, and other surface irregularities. Where small test holes or narrow trenches have been made with shovels in an area cleared by the road patrol, these should be filled in before the machine again travels over the surface; otherwise, the wheels may drop into them, thus tilting the blade and dropping loose dirt at one end while the other end gouges unevenly below the desired grade.

As in any other sort of digging, close controls are essential here to forestall partial or complete eradication of the evidence in situ and the obscuring of associations. An accurate surface contour map should be made before the machinery goes to work, and fixed datum points should be established. Thereafter, vertical controls can be readily maintained in the form of narrow unexcavated strips paralleling the sweeps of the machinery; the edges of these strips, smoothed by means of shovels or other implements, will provide adequate stratigraphic sections from ground surface to whatever depth is reached by the blade.

Given a competent, experienced, and interested machine operator, an adequate machine in good condition, and an experienced supervisor who will check on progress at all stages of the operations, there is no doubt in my mind that the advantages of such mechanized work greatly outweigh the disadvantages. A certain amount of specimen breakage or loss and the occasional loss of other data concerning features and associations will have to be reckoned with. It has been our experience, however, that very few specimens or features suffer seriously from the weight of the machinery on reasonably firm ground so long as the ground is not churned by wheels or track. From personal observation and from inquiry of those in direct charge of operations, I doubt that there is any more actual destruction or obscuring of evidence where power machinery is properly used under careful supervision than where any large crew of untrained or perhaps uninterested laborers is employed. At Medicine Creek in 1948, I took occasion several times to examine the dumps closely after washing rains, and I am satisfied that no more cultural material was apparent here than could be found in the wake of many of the larger CWA or PWA excavating crews of the 1930's. Moreover, the relatively small amount of material and information that may be lost by not scrutinizing every ounce of dirt through hand operations is overbalanced by the vastly greater quantities of ground that can be explored through machine operations. Among the several professional archaeologists who at one time or another participated in or viewed the operations at Medicine Creek, at Angostura, and at Fort Randall not one, so far as I know, seriously questioned the long-run gains to be realized from these methods.

Earth-moving machinery is not the answer, of course, to all the problems of archaeological excavation. There are many types of sites in which its use would be very limited or wholly inadvisable, just as in any site there comes a time when the machine should be used only for removal of backdirt or for further exploratory trenching. Caves and rock shelters, middens under close stratigraphic study, cemeteries, house sites, cache pits, and similar features demanding continuous scrutiny and painstaking work are no place for a bulldozer. As in the case of some village sites or camp levels, where there is an exceptionally rich or unique artifact content in the contemporary ground surface, power machinery may do more harm than good. An area strewn with large boulders or containing many coarse cobblestones, or a wooded tract with stumps and standing trees would offer serious obstacles to a road patrol and would doubtless prevent a bulldozer from cutting a smooth, even face. In sandy or loose soils damage from the wheels or tracks would perhaps be a fairly serious matter.

Most archaeologists work in the field with sadly inadequate funds and perforce are able to do little more than sample their sites except through a continuing program. It might be objected, therefore, that the purchase of a bulldozer or road patrol is out of the question because of the cost. This is undoubtedly true; there are on the market small machines costing not much more than a pickup truck, but their ability to do what an archaeological project might demand from time to time is still undemonstrated. Even the rental charges on a medium-sized bulldozer, at say five to ten dollars per hour, would in course of several weeks eat deeply into the budget of most field projects. Still, in any site where removal of overburden or cutting of exploratory trenches promises to absorb much of the available time and manpower, a few hours or days of work with a bulldozer or road patrol will accomplish more than several dozen men with shovels could do in weeks. In any reasonably large-scale operation on open village sites or buried occupation zones, money used to hire a machine will be money well spent.

Certain technical aspects of the power-machinery problem have not been discussed here, partly because I am not qualified to comment on them and partly because our experience is yet too limited to draw on for useful leads. In the Missouri River Basin considerable thought has been given to the advisability of acquiring small bulldozers of either wheeled or crawler type; their transportation, maintenance, and operation would presumably offer fewer worries than would the larger machines used by contractors and construction agencies. Since, however, such machines are much lighter, it seems wiser to wait until actual field trials have shown whether they have the necessary power and stamina to do sod breaking and other heavy tasks.

Other problems to be worked out include a determination of the most efficient ratio between men and machines, assuming that the archaeologist has a choice among several machines of different types. This ratio, obviously, will be quite variable since it will depend on factors that differ from one project or site to another.

From the results so far achieved at sites of rather varied character in the Missouri River Basin, it seems certain that heavy earth-moving equipment can play a highly important and generally successful part in the even more comprehensive excavations that will have to be undertaken in the next few years. The five huge main-stem dams —Gavins Point, Fort Randall, Big Bend, Oahe, and Garrison—under construction or in prospect for the Missouri River between Yankton, South Dakota, and Williston, North Dakota, will completely obliterate many hundreds of sites. At most of these, scientific investigations, if they have been made at all, have been on a very small scale, including the collecting of samples of surface materials and occasionally limited test trenching or the opening of one or a few house sites. That as many as a half dozen village sites have been adequately sampled to date is doubtful; not one, large or small, has ever been investigated as thoroughly as were the Medicine Creek sites in 1948. Yet here are the basic data from which alone several centuries of culture growth and development by a number of historic tribes may be reconstructed. There seems scant prospect that within the time remaining before completion of the water-control program enough manpower can be brought to bear here to salvage even a minimum amount of the data we must have. Unless archaeologists are to content themselves with watching most of their raw materials go under water, I believe that the large-scale application of heavy earth-moving equipment plus all available manpower is the only real and effective solution to the dilemma. Although actual field trials have yet to be made with mechanized techniques in this area, those of us who watched the Medicine Creek work are convinced that the same sort of operations would pay off handsomely on the large village sites and other remains of the upper Missouri. It is equally certain that at most other water-control projects throughout the Missouri Basin where archaeological salvage work is called for, and where in many cases overburden removal and the handling of large quantities of low-yield material is a major factor in planning, mechanized archaeology would be as rewarding and economical a procedure as anything of a practical nature yet devised.

I am aware that the proposal to include earth-moving machinery as a routine item of equipment in work that all of us were trained to do in the most meticulous fashion we know may cause some lifted eyebrows. The time remaining for archaeological salvage in many localities throughout our land is, however, tragically short; therefore, as between nibbling away interminably at one or two sites with shovels, trowels, camel's-hair brushes, and orangewood sticks and, alternatively, working out a half dozen or a dozen sites with the aid of power machinery, I think there is only one answer. It is my considered opinion, also, that anyone who has the eye-opening experience we have had and who can find the wherewithal will give serious consideration to the use of earth-moving equipment wherever opportunity allows, whether or not an emergency like the present one exists.

DISCUSSION

COLLIER: What was the maximum depth taken off by the bulldozers on that Nebraska site?

WEDEL: In the village site excavations supervised by River Basin personnel, the overburden seldom exceeded two to three feet. At Lime Creek the University of Nebraska State Museum used explosives and a bulldozer to remove upwards of thirty-five feet of overburden.

GRIFFIN: Didn't we see moving pictures of that excavation by the bulldozer? Were those moving pictures or were they kodachromes?

WEDEL: You may have seen both.

GRIFFIN: If that film could be duplicated and distributed to various centers so that people could see that type of excavation being made, it would be a very effective demonstration.

WEDEL: One rather effective way to do archaeological

exploration in that region is to ride on the cab of a road patrol, above and immediately behind the blade. You can then watch the fresh cut. In the work at Medicine Creek we could work theoretically anywhere in the reservoir area with the machinery; actually, we were more or less obligated to stay within the lower two or three miles. The practice there became one of stripping overburden off a proven archaeological zone, putting the men to work on that area with shovel and trowel, and then sending the road patrol with the operator and perhaps one observer up the valley along the bluffs to sweep off every little point or terrace to which they came. In the course of a day or two, it was possible to do a more thorough job of scouting the area by machine than a crew of several dozen men could do in weeks or months.

COLLIER: The area was one on which you previously had no information?

WEDEL: That's right. Often the areas tested were simply small points on which you might find a potsherd or two, or perhaps a few chips, but we didn't know what might be present underground in the way of structures or other features.

RITCHIE: I'm wondering how the idea of using power machinery would be greeted by landowners, say in the East, in cultivated fields and places where they might consider it excessively damaging to the property. It seems to me that if you brought in machinery of any kind to sites situated on farm lands in many parts of the country, you'd be turned down on those grounds.

JOHNSON: You get turned down many times without bringing in machinery.

WEDEL: At Medicine Creek and elsewhere we didn't have to worry about that problem. The sites in the future pool area will soon be covered anyway, and the landowners presumably have been reimbursed for loss of the land. With the road patrol, however, you don't need to tear up the land seriously; you simply push the dirt to one side so that it can be replaced if necessary. By careful planning the same procedure could be worked out for the bulldozer, even where fairly large areas were to be stripped.

GRIFFIN: I should think that it's better to do it that way if the topsoil does not have artifact material in it. You then remove the topsoil and put it off to one side. When you've dug the site, you put the topsoil back again. That's a lot better than miscellaneous pit digging. You actually have an arguable point that the bulldozer has an advantage over traditional digging techniques.

JOHNSON: I think you'd have quite an argument with New England farmers because what topsoil they have in New England is pretty sacred. It's a good idea, Jimmy, but New England farmers are rather fussy about their topsoil.

BREW: One of the best sites that the Massachusetts Archaeological Society dug was found because a farmer was selling his topsoil. If we had gone in with a bulldozer, he would have been very happy.

Obviously, this thing steps up our personal relations, which are always important. Then there's another aspect to this; out in the Southwest where we've always used teams and scrapers and scoops previously for removing backfill, it's hard to believe that we've reached the stage where we can go in, as we did last year, where there aren't any horses left. There you're faced with the necessity of using power machinery just for removing your backfill, and there is no power machinery that is located close by except that used by the county road crews. It's necessary to get a reasonable liaison in advance. The way it works is that in the course of a summer there will be a man who comes in on contract to certain ranches for a short period and then moves on somewhere else. If you keep in contact with the farmers, you can find out when somebody with power machinery is due in the country and can make arrangements in advance to get your few hours or days when the machinery is there. In most areas in the Southwest the power machinery is available only once in the course of a summer. You've got to find out about it when the machine is there, or else you're just out of luck.

WEDEL: In the Medicine Creek work we had an unusually good break in that the machinery was there practically all the time we needed it. It cost the River Basin Surveys nothing. Ordinarily, I understand, the road patrol rents for about ten dollars an hour; the bulldozer varies from five to ten. In the course of the five months, or twenty-one weeks, that we had machinery at work at Medicine Creek, the Bureau of Reclamation figured its total cost at about $2,000 for operating one machine.

BRAINERD: What sort of co-operation did you get?

WEDEL: The Bureau of Reclamation furnished all the labor, the labor foreman, and machinery with operator. The River Basin Surveys provided only the two men for supervision of the archaeological aspects of the operation.

BRAINERD: Is that rather general?

WEDEL: That particular arrangement came about through the enlightened and co-operative attitude of the Bureau of Reclamation, its regional director in Denver, and the chairman of the Interior Missouri Basin Field Committee, Mr. W. G. Sloan. Whether the same thing can be worked out again elsewhere, I don't know. We've made some efforts to interest the Army engineers on the upper Missouri, where such co-operative projects would be the ideal setup, but to date the engineers have not come through on anything like Reclamation's assistance at Medicine Creek.

SPAULDING: Is that all operator work?

WEDEL: So far as the engineers are concerned, the only prospect for work is in the immediate vicinity of a dam, where they might be willing to make their machinery available when it is not otherwise needed. We can't be sure whether that means a week at a time, or only thirty minutes between other jobs.

FORD: Did you ever try using a carryall?

WEDEL: Only once, and that not by plan. The boys found one deep house site in an area that had been stripped. We had given it up, and the construction crews were working at top speed all around; one of the operators of a carryall offered to clear the house site for our people. They gave him some indication of its probable depth, and he cleaned out most of the remaining fill in two sweeps. In perhaps an hour's time, the whole job was finished; it would have taken the men alone the better part of a day or even more.

RITCHIE: What would you think of the use of a trencher, in testing for pits or graves, that could be set at any depth to cut, without disturbing the whole terrain, a series of narrow trenches across a field? Have you ever used one?

WEDEL: We have never used one, but it might be very useful in connection with Missouri Valley and other sites for cross trenching rapidly on a large scale.

RITCHIE: I would think that in agricultural land there might be less objection to the use of a small, light, powered trencher than to the cutting away of the whole topsoil. It would accomplish much the same results for our purposes, namely, discover the principal features with a minimum expenditure of time and effort.

WEDEL: I think it has real possibilities, and, as with some of the other power tools, we're just hoping for a chance somewhere along the line to give them a thorough test. Certainly, the road patrol and the bulldozer will work; I have no doubt that there are other machines that could be used to good advantage.

RITCHIE: Some of these machines are light enough to put on small trailers drawn by a station wagon or a jeep.

WEDEL: Yes, but I don't think that light tractors are likely to be very practical.

RITCHIE: Ditchers might be.

BREW: There is one factor with regard to these light tractors which I don't believe you've mentioned: those which come in a size which will fit the usual archaeological budget are dangerous. Farmers find them so, too. They have a tendency to turn over rather easily, particularly in the hands of untrained or unskilled operators such as you are likely to have.

COLLIER: There's another situation where machinery might be used to advantage, that is, in large stratified midden sites in which the artifact content is extremely low, and ordinary digging methods don't yield large enough samples and hence do not give an accurate picture of historical changes. I

have in mind the middens in the Aleutian Islands. With some
kind of machinery you could move a lot of dirt, but you'd
also have to devise some mechanical means of sifting the
material and getting the artifacts out. In areas like the
Aleutians, unless you're able to have hundreds of men working, you never get a very good picture because the sample
is much smaller than from the usual cultural deposits.

WEDEL: We had hoped for a chance in 1949 to test some
of the larger village sites on the upper Missouri by simply
running bulldozers at right angles each way through a village,
making deep profile cuts through the site, and then working
back from those. This technique could be used as well in
shell heaps or middens. Once you have your initial cut or
cuts down to clean soil, and thus some indication as to the
depth and extent of the archaeological zone, further excavations can be planned and carried out far more effectively.

COLLIER: Have you ever investigated a mechanical or
power screen?

WEDEL: No, we've never done that.

COOK: I'd like to ask you if you think this power machinery
would be applicable to the type of site we have in California,
which consists mainly of mounds above the level surface of
the ground, of rather soft material, completely loaded with
artifacts and burials. Do you think you'd destroy more than
you'd get?

WEDEL: I'm inclined to think you would, at any rate if you
removed the entire deposit by machine. The principal advantage I can see for it in that connection — I'm thinking in
terms of salvage operations at one or two of the California
shell heaps into which I have sunk a spade — would be to run
an initial trench through it, regardless of lost or damaged
specimens, then work back to the sides of the trench. Thus,
you still get your stratigraphy on each side and also your
sample artifacts, but there would be no floundering around all
summer digging by shovel and wondering what was at the
bottom or where the bottom was. You'd know at the end of
the first day or two where and what it was and could then
proceed accordingly.

Collaboration Among Scientific Fields with Special Reference to Archaeology

Frederick Johnson

At the present time there is a fortunate tendency to break down the barriers which formerly segregated fields of science into rather discrete compartments. We are familiar with the idea of research teams made up of people representing such disciplines as economics, various phases of the social sciences, medicine, and a multitude of other subjects. The investigations of many of these teams often emphasize contemporary culture existing as it always has in a complex and composite milieu. The development of collaborations including archaeology is relatively recent except for the long-standing and widely-recognized relationship between archaeology and geology. In its beginning phases archaeology was concerned, in the main, with isolated collections of things. The modern trend, however, is toward studies of culture and culture history in the broader anthropological sense. If research teams can study contemporary culture or aspects of it, it is logical to employ appropriate disciplines, including archaeology, in order to investigate culture at a sequence of points in time.

It is useful to consider the general background of joint endeavors to solve archaeological problems, for such collaborations have paved the way for future, more extensive group investigations. If we can more fully understand the manner in which contributions from archaeology, physiography, climatology, and various phases of biology have been combined for the purpose of solving a problem, we may be able to develop more useful collaborations. Also, the knowledge and understanding gained in this way will facilitate the needed inclusions of data from other disciplines.

There is no need to dwell on the fact that as archaeology sloughed off the antiquarianism of its early days it became more closely integrated with various fields in anthropology. Now there is an ever-broadening area in which problems are of mutual concern to archaeologists, ethnographers, linguists, and others. One of the most prominent characteristics of archaeology, the one which most effectively differentiates it from its sister fields in anthropology, is the location of its basic data and the methods used in making collections.

The material relics of human culture are found in deposits of many sorts. The deposits vary in kind from those deep in the ground to those on the surface of some manmade mound or building. Buildings are of as much importance as the relics they may enclose. Furthermore, any possible variation in kind of deposit may be found in any kind of situation, from open prairie to forest or jungle or in an almost inaccessible cave. Deposits may be buried or exposed either through natural agencies or by the hands of contemporary or succeeding generations of men. As a result, archaeologists are concerned with sequences of deposits which may be correlated with events in human history or in the development of the surface of the land. More frequently than not, the remains of human culture, having been deposited through time by a complicated concatenation of circumstances, are not found in "levels" which are easily identifiable by means of the characteristics of the materials themselves or by the manner of their deposition. Nevertheless, they exist in continua and thus the levels marked off by archaeologists actually represent the opinions of the investigator. The fact that levels and continua do exist, together with the probability that once man reached a given region human occupation was never again interrupted except for periods during which the area was rendered uninhabitable, is of significance from the points of view of many other sciences. These complexities, of course, constitute one of the main subjects of archaeological study. The determination by excavation of the order of the deposits and also the proper handling of the recovered material are our principle pride and the measure of our skill.

The superposition levels or continua, each having its characteristic archaeological content, give rise to a sequence or stratigraphy. From such sequences it is possible to deduce the major part of the historical data which are essential to all archaeological work. It is important to emphasize the obvious: humans left their remains upon a surface of the earth. It is essential to determine and understand the properties of this surface if human life and culture are to be fully interpreted. Purely archaeological techniques and methods can provide but a modicum of the necessary data. Much can be learned, however, from scientists who are otherwise concerned with these surfaces. Commonly, specialists in geology, biology, pollen analysis, and soil science have been consulted in order to explain the nature of the surface upon which the archaeological data rest; however, there are, presumably, other specialists who can also contribute useful background data.

It is important to recognize that each scientific field, including archaeology, has objectives which can be defined with varying degrees of precision. These are the bases for every separate attack, and they provide the background for the definition of problems. In order that one attack may contribute to another, a common ground must be found. Seldom does an outline of a specific problem involve basic tenets of various scientific fields. Rather, this mutual significance appears as problems are outlined and broadened. For example, given an ideal stratigraphic situation where archaeological materials are found in distinct "levels" separated by sterile strata, the archaeologist produces descriptions of the characteristics of each "level" which may be interpreted as a sequence of occupations differing or not as the case may be. If sufficient distributional data are available, numerous conclusions concerning the people and their culture may be drawn. The geologist who is collaborating is interested in the origin and development of the beds which constitute the "levels" and in their surfaces for purely geological reasons which involve only rudimentary and generalized consideration of the human occupation. The mutual problem includes the part man played in the chronology and paleogeography of the region. At first sight the area of collaboration in this simplified situation may seem small and somewhat one-sided. It is true, however, that the archaeological data may contribute considerably to geological hypotheses. For example, the cultural material may impose time limits on the chronological estimates, and also the aboriginal economy defined by the cultural material will contribute to opinions concerning the detailed environment and general geography of the period.

The above perhaps oversimplified remarks may serve as background for a point which must never be forgotten. Every field of science exists because of a hard core of fact which is the subject of specific research. The existence and validity of this core must be recognized by every one during the debate which is the inevitable result of the attempt to correlate archaeological and other sorts of information. Surrounding this core, however, is a penumbra of data and hypothesis which is not completely comprehensible until it has been the subject of appropriate, interlocking research by specialists in other sciences.

The noun collaboration comes from the verb "to collaborate," which Webster defines as "to labor together; to work or act jointly, as in writing or study." In order that a collaboration among a group of scientists may be successful, they must actually "labor together." One very important aspect of this is the mutual understanding of problems of the various fields including specific objectives which may not be entirely pertinent to the projected study. There can be no greater aid to a collaboration than the possession by the participants of, as a minimum, a sympathetic understanding of at least the theoretical background of the fields involved. Such an understanding indicates the range of the subject matter and the limitations of the results, and makes possible the mutual understanding of the methodology used by each participant. An archaeologist, for example, must understand why a collaborating botanist, in order to prepare himself to discuss the ethnobotany of a site, clambers up a mountain to pull flowers up by the roots, and the botanist should be informed of the necessity and need for the painfully precise archaeological excavations with trowel, knife, and brush.

For mutual understanding it is elemental that a clear statement of various aspects of the problem be made for joint use. It is essential that this be set forth in the simplest of the king's English. Many criticisms of scientific jargon have been made, and semantic monstrosities often obscure an astounding ignorance. The attempt to make a clear statement of a problem can present a real difficulty if there is no precedent to follow, or no previous experience on the part of the participants, as is often the case.

Another point is that an archaeologist, or any one else for that matter, should not present his collaborating colleague with a mass of samples or specimens and a sheaf of undigested field notes and expect him to answer all, or even a few, questions. To do this is to expect a miracle, and furthermore this is the opposite of the idea of collaboration. It is desirable that collaborators work together in the field. Such labors do not necessarily add specific details but they do provide an invaluable point of view. For example, when an archaeologist climbs out of his trench to spend time ranging the country with his colleague who is a geologist, the minute details in the profile appear in a perspective which enhances their significance (sometimes their insignificance) in a startling manner. It is true also that work in the field, when combined in this way, will open new lines of attack. While data are being collected, it is often possible by trial and error, if by no other way, to modify the several lines of investigation so that the field work will keep pace with steadily expanding problems. If left until the close of a field season, the analysis of several sets of field notes brings to light inevitable lacunae preventing the development of ideas which in a field collaboration would have been investigated on the spot.

The collaboration must be carried through all the steps in the research. The participants must understand how each one processes his data and compiles the results. In each of these stages the interchange of ideas is essential, and the success of the venture depends largely upon a mutual understanding and tolerance of everyone's trials and tribulations.

Comments on the details of collaboration between scientific fields can be of only the most generalized sort. The reason for this lies in the fact that each problem in which collaboration is potentially possible includes peculiar theoretical and practical factors. These vary considerably, and an attempt to describe them briefly could well imply limitations which do not exist. The important thing, as far as archaeology is concerned, is to tie the cultural objects to a bed or horizon by careful excavation. Also, the archaeologist should prove that objects of the same sort lie in such a bed at as many locations as may be found. It must be proved, in addition, that the cultural materials do not occur in any other beds in the region in a manner which vitiates conclusions based on the primary site under consideration. It is not possible here to discuss the definition of a region, but it may be pointed out that the boundaries will be elusive and at best empirical. In the end, the region will be in large measure determined by limitations of time and funds and by arbitrary agreement among the participants. Thus, the boundaries will be a compromise, in part practical and in part between definitions of the various fields involved.

Dr. Kirk Bryan has stated a number of conditions which must be met before collaboration between geology and archaeology may be successful. These may be listed as follows: (1) Cultural objects must be associated with a definite bed or beds. (2) These beds must be related to some definite local event. (3) This event must be related to other events or be of wide geographic extent. (4) This event and related events must also be related to some geologic chronology.[1] It is obvious that archaeological work can never determine whether or not all these conditions exist. Adequate archaeological work, however, should produce data on the first of these conditions, which may indicate whether or not geological examination is likely to be productive. The term "adequate archaeological work" implies not only knowledge of the details discovered during the excavation of a site or series of sites, but a well-founded knowledge of the geography of the region in which the sites are located. Such knowledge must come from observations on the ground, for no literature will provide all the data desired.

The background for the above remarks is the type of geological work which can be done in areas where deposits may be traced over appreciable distances. That there are many other situations is obvious. In coastal regions, for example, the sites may be in beds related to the fluctuation of sea level. Such sites require the employment of special geological methods. The study of the location of cultural materials in caves has characteristics which have been well described.

The age of cave deposits is a problem that can rarely be solved by a direct attack. In general... cave deposits have no physical connection with any deposits in the locality beyond the cave mouth. Hence, the sequence of events recorded in the cave is not directly connected with other sequences that took place outside its limited and special space.... Usually, however, general arguments are the only recourse in attempts to date cave deposits. The contained human or animal remains may afford a partial or complete correlation with known geologic horizons.... If, however, the cave deposits can be interpreted as representing a sequence of events related to or in part the result of climatic fluctuations, an independent line of inquiry is available. The climatic implications of cave deposits may be related to the rhythm of climatic fluctuations of the past. Thus a connection may be made with a general and world-wide chronology—the pulsations of climate characteristic of the Pleistocene.[2]

---

[1] Cf. discussion in Bryan and Ray, 1940.
[2] Bryan, 1941, pp. 45-46.

Given the possibility of accomplishing geological work in collaboration with archaeology under the above conditions or under many others not mentioned, it remains to outline the character of the resulting contribution. In some instances geochronological "dates" are purely and simply estimates. In others the estimates are based on knowledge from both fields, often combined with biological data, derived from the analysis of pollen and other researches. The difficulty geologists have in estimating dates having a range of accuracy useful to archaeologists will persist for a long while. The reason for this is that for geological purposes broad estimates are useful and satisfactory. Dates determined for archaeological work are in a sense special cases requiring additional and, in the judgment of many geologists, needless labor. Because of this difficulty geologists are sometimes reluctant to take up a project where short periods of time are involved. This reluctance is frequently an initial reaction, however, and it may be reversed if the full significance of the basic problem can be clearly stated.

Another contribution geology can make to the understanding of human culture, including its distribution, has been called "paleogeography." The late Dr. Kirk Bryan has presented his idea of this concept in an unpublished manuscript. The attempt at definition made here is a summary based on some discussion with him and is perhaps not as broad and complete as it should be. Moraines, lake beds, outwash deposits, soil phenomena, layers of silt, and all the other innumerable types of deposits and topographic features which are the stock in trade of geologists are evidence of past events. It is usually possible to determine from these events, especially sequences of them, factors which describe the general and often the specific environment, defined in its broadest sense, existing at any one time and particularly at the time represented by the bed associated with human remains. More often than not, these environmental factors are basic ones, that is, they provide an essential background for further refinements as, for instance, the nature of contemporary vegetation, a paleobotanical study. It is clear that paleogeography contributes to a knowledge of the environment at any past time and hence to human ecology. This in itself is essential to the understanding of human culture. It may be noted that knowledge of human activities as determined in archaeological work is of equal importance to facts from other sciences in the determination of environmental factors. That is, the ability to determine the economics of a group of people from their artifacts is a unique archaeological contribution of increasing precision and value. The presence of certain types of culture is an indication, at least within broad limits, of the character of the environments in which a group existed. Archaeological inferences of this sort should be integrated into paleogeographic inferences based upon geological and botanical facts.

The degree to which collaborations with geologists may be organized depends largely upon existing geological knowledge. If this is not adequate as a background, archaeologists must be prepared to aid geological projects, the value of which, either to geology or archaeology, can only be measured in future possibilities. This is suggested because such projects may have no relationship to current geological work and, if undertaken, may require that other projects be postponed or even abandoned. There has been some unfortunate criticism leveled at geologists, and at other scientists as a matter of fact, for their reluctance to work on studies of immediate value to archaeology. Before passing such judgments archaeologists and their colleagues should acquaint themselves with problems in each other's fields and thus be prepared either to understand the difficulties involved or to arrange the projected work so that it may have broader value.

There are reasons for suggesting that although collaborations with biology have been successful, not as much information and help have been received as is possible. Archaeologists may not have been persistent enough in their discussions with biologists, or, if they were, the biologists may not have available exactly the type of data most needed. It is archaeological custom to have bones, shells, vegetal material, and the like identified. All too often the identifications of these materials are relegated to an appendix and only bare mention of them is made in the discussion. Lacking such discussions, the lists are of little or no value and are hardly worth the trouble caused the collaborating biologists. If the significance of these lists of identified materials is adequately discussed by sympathetic biologists, contributions to the results of the whole endeavor will be inevitable. It must be noted that defeats in this type of collaboration are by no means general and that interrelations of value both to biology and archaeology are steadily increasing. The identification of Pleistocene vertebrates and the increasing knowledge of their ecology and the sequence of Pleistocene faunas is one case in point. Studies of the extinction of animals have also provided a certain perspective.

The significance of the presence of wild plants in cultural levels is less well known, but the importance of the provenience and distribution of edible and domesticated plants is receiving a great deal of much-needed attention. One aspect of biological work can be employed to much greater advantage. Archaeologists should stimulate more than they do now researches in geographic botany and similar fields in zoology. No criticism is intended or implied, for such would be presumptuous in the extreme, but it is unfortunately true that ecological and even chronological data of a sort useful in archaeology, geology, and other fields are either lacking or far from complete. The reasons for this situation are complicated ones in which archaeology is an innocent bystander.[3] An archaeologist must know something about the problems of geographic botany so that he may limit the range of his discussions and evaluate the botanical results. There have been instances, however, when rather complete botanical data have either been available or have been secured during the course of field collaborations. These relatively rare studies are valuable from the point of view of method, if for no other reason, and they can serve as the background against which problems of wide scope and use to investigators in several fields may be outlined.[4]

Pollen analysis, or to give it its new name, palynology, is an interesting field of research because of necessity it partakes of the nature of a collaboration.[5] It is a stratigraphic study in which layers are identified by pollen content, by botanical, zoological, and archaeological inclusions, by geological and limnological character, and by several other means or a combination of them. The wide range of data included has made it difficult even to supply a satisfactory name to the endeavor. This heterogeneous character is in part responsible for a lack of basic premises which are completely satisfactory. Pollen spectra have been assumed to indicate fluctuations in climate. By correlating actual archaeological finds in peat and also various events of geological or other nature with points on curves representing these climatic fluctuations, dates have been obtained. The validity of the dates of climatic

[3] Cf. Raup, 1942, pp. 319-54.
[4] Cf. Raup and Johnson, n.d.
[5] Erdtman, 1943.

fluctuations obtained by this hard and incredibly detailed work is subject to some doubt, particularly in the finer details. These doubts cannot be removed from what is certainly a valuable tool unless archaeologists, geologists, botanists, and all others concerned increase the amount of their collaboration. This criticism applies to the American field. In a more limited sense it also applies to European studies. In spite of the great and extremely good and valuable work which has been done on the Old World, [6] it is still necessary to perfect the basic premises of palynology. It behooves scientists to make certain that pollen analysts are applying criteria of various fields correctly and, furthermore, that the basic tenets are logically sound.

Elsewhere in this volume there is an account of the method of dating ancient materials by means of radiocarbon. [7] This is a particularly apt example of a type of collaboration. By supplying samples dated archaeologically within a range of accuracy less than the range of error of the method it was possible for physicists to test rather significant hypotheses concerning radioactivity. On the other hand, the method, a product of research in physics, will make it necessary for archaeologists to review the methods used in stratigraphic studies at their sites. Such a critical review will inevitably lead to an improvement in field observation and description. It is true also that methods of collecting materials and the record concerning them will be improved, for even under the present circumstances the degree of precision needed in locating and preserving specimens for Carbon^{14} analysis is greater than is frequently used in archaeological excavations.

Much has been omitted during the foregoing remarks on various aspects of collaboration. Little has been said, for instance, concerning the theoretical and philosophical basis for an integrated approach to a problem. There are also important factors which are practical rather than intellectual. In a collaborative attack matters pertaining to the reporting of the results are as important in their way as is the joint research. Great emphasis has been placed by some workers upon the desirability of having reports appear in the literature of the respective scientific fields. Although the reasons for this have some validity, close adherence to the idea serves

---

[6]Cf. Zeuner, 1946, for an outline of palynology.

[7]See Collier, this volume, pp. 97-101.

only to retard the broadening of research programs. It is desirable, if not necessary, to compile final archaeological reports in such a way that they include all steps taken toward the solution of problems. The advantages of "laboring together" must be carried over onto the printed page. Separation of the results makes it difficult to document even a summary discussion so that a reader may fully understand the background for the conclusions, or to form a satisfactory judgment concerning hypotheses. An example of a liberal policy in publication is furnished by the two reports on the Boylston Street Fishweir.[8] I would hesitate to mention them except that others helped me preserve in unified publications the results of two complicated collaborations. The study of Grassy Island is another similar example.[9]

Collaborations are frequently organized about a problem which develops either while investigation in a single field is under way, or because in the beginning it is known that a detailed knowledge of the location of an artifact-bearing bed will be required. As the organization progresses the character of the final analysis must be kept in mind. There should be no hesitation in planning for the publication of a report which will include all phases of the work. In addition to the value of such a unified and comprehensive report the person initiating the collaboration encourages his colleagues to proceed. Outlets for publication in almost every field are never completely adequate, and the promise of full and early publication of the results of research can be a great incentive There is another point. Work in an allied field which is stimulated by archaeological discussion is not always easily classified. Editors are sometimes critical of single papers emanating from a collaboration simply because the real reason for the form and content is not apparent. Such papers are out of their context; they belong in a collaborative report.

It is recognized, of course, that the reports of several collaborators will contain a great deal of material which is not directly applicable to the problem at hand. In fact, some of this material may be so far afield as to appear irrelevant. This should be no deterrent to publication, for it is certain that such data are necessary for the final argument; also they will be of value or use in analogous studies. The problem of distributing this knowledge in appropriate places, that is, in the literatures of the various fields, is largely a bibliographic

[8] Johnson, et al, 1942, 1949.   [9] Johnson and Raup, 1947.

one. Summaries, book reviews, and simple notices together with adequate library record provide cross references for this material. Furthermore, such cross referencing can result in the broadening of the area in which scholars browse in libraries, a fact which is of value in itself.

A final observation is in the way of an appeal to archaeologists based on an idea which has been implied in almost every one of the foregoing paragraphs. As archaeologists, and certainly as other research workers, too, concentrate on the details of their specific researches, they must never lose sight of the place these occupy and their eventual significance in science. It is becoming increasingly obvious that archaeology cannot answer all the questions concerning human culture and its history which archaeological work brings to light. There are aspects of archaeological discoveries which can only be fully explained by parallel researches. In order that archaeologists of the future may make better use of existing potentialities and those which will be added in the future, it seems certain that students should be more broadly trained. Such training is discussed in other papers in this volume.

DISCUSSION

WARD: I would like to emphasize the enormous importance of geological evidence for the archaeology of the Old World. A time scale of appalling length has to be established for prehistoric man in the Old World. Man, insofar as we can tell of his existence by means of his artifacts, must have begun just about at the beginning of the Pleistocene period, five hundred thousand or a million years or so ago. Obviously, the only reliable time scale that we can use in such a vast period is a geological scale and, particularly in western Europe, one based on glacial evidence. Most geologists, unfortunately, regard the Pleistocene as such a recent period that they are not much interested in it. We have to get the geologists and lasso them and convert a few of them to interest in our problems. There is plenty of evidence, in the form of glacial moraines, river terraces, and raised beaches, all of which have some connection with one another. Yet I know personally of only three cases where real correlation of archaeological remains with actual phases of glaciation has been established. One case, of course, is in this country, at

Lindenmeier, the work of Bryan and Ray:[10] another case is in India, the work of de Terra and Paterson;[11] and work on the third case was started recently by Movius and Bryan at La Colombiere in the upper Rhone Valley in France.[12]

All the textbooks, it is true, have nice little schemes of paleolithic cultures, and each one is assigned to an interglacial period or subdivision of the Pleistocene, but this is all based on pure guess work because man didn't build his huts on the edge of the retreating ice sheet, and it requires careful field work to determine the age of the horizons in which human artifacts occur. Such field work is very necessary. There was a suggestion that a major job might be done in the Rhone Valley, which would have one end in the Alpine moraines and the other in the raised beaches of the Mediterranean, with a study of the connecting river terraces, but that's such a large project that it probably never will be undertaken. Still, I hope that a great deal more in the way of geological dating will be done in the Old World, following the methods used in the Lindenmeier project.

RITCHIE: It seems to me, Fred, that in dealing with the relatively short time periods with which most of us work, say a few thousand years, the geologist is not of much use to us. At least I have found it so in a number of cases in which I have tried to get aid from geologists. The results have been negligible. For example, right now, in the Hudson Valley we have a site under a fair amount of sterile material, embedded in a clay that rests on a glacial hardpan. I have had several geologists there, including a man from the U.S. Geologic Survey and a specialist in Pleistocene and Recent geology of the Hudson area, no two of whom have agreed except for the identification of the basic clay as glacial. That's the kind of result I have had over and over again in my work. Evidently the geological techniques for such recent dating are just not available.

JOHNSON: It depends a good deal upon the area; also, it depends a good deal upon your men. Geologists, especially in the East, who are interested in the details of postglacial events are very rare. We were lucky in having Kirk Bryan at Harvard, and Richard Flint at Yale has some interest in local problems. The details of the glaciation and its retreat

---

[10] Bryan and Ray, 1940. [11] de Terra and Paterson, 1939. [12] Movius, 1949.

COLLABORATION AMONG SCIENTIFIC FIELDS 47

are being worked out. For example, in the fishweir study we have dealt with three moraines, relatively small deposits, and all three are post-Mankato. Probably they could be correlated with some of the deposits which you have in the upper Hudson, that is, they may be due to little oscillations in the retreating stages of the glaciation. We are able to tie some of these deposits at the fishweir to these moraines.

The development of a collaboration depends on the man whom you approach. When I started in with the fishweir, the geologists, even Kirk Bryan himself, said: "This is very swell, very interesting, but it is unlikely that anything can be done about it." It was only necessary to define the geological problem roughly and generally. That is, there were fishweir stakes about fifteen feet below sea level, and layers of different silts could be identified. Eventually, we were able to argue on the probability that the fishweir stakes were in a geological context which might be approachable. The whole problem involved other things, such as the status of knowledge of New England geology. In addition, there was the problem of finding a trained student to do the job.

RITCHIE: All I've been able to get is that in certain instances the elapsed time span is to be measured in terms of millenniums, rather than centuries, but no correlations with widespread events are possible.

JOHNSON: Well, of course, you have those difficulties. It all depends on the detail which can be supplied and which can be used to modify a first guess concerning chronology.

WEDEL: There is some evidence, I think, that as regards the last few thousand years, the geologist is apt to get more help out of the archaeologist than vice versa. Out in the West, up until ten to fifteen years ago, the geologist or physiographer would look at a buried soil surface and toss off a guess-date like ten thousand years ago. Then the archaeologists began to pick pottery or other materials out of various buried soils, and now they find that the better geologists out there are much more cautious when questioned about the age of something like that. First of all, they usually inquire whether you have found anything that can be dated by other methods.

JOHNSON: Of course, that's the function of collaboration;

there's a give and take in collaborating with geologists or with any other scientists, for that matter. The thing is to maintain your integrity as an archaeologist. For instance, you take pottery out of a soil which a geologist says is ten thousand years old. You can finally convince any reasonable person that pottery is archaeologically datable and that it is recent. Eventually, any scientist will revise his hypotheses to include such facts.

MATSON: There are other techniques which might be applicable. A fairly new one in geology is sedimentary petrography, in which the orientation and interrelation of the mineral grains are studied. This is a very detailed, time consuming process, but one which produces worth-while results. One of the outstanding men of this field, P. D. Krynine, of Pennsylvania State, made a preliminary study of some of Movius' soil samples from Burma.[13] Krynine has been saving the rest of the soil samples for his graduate students, but none of them are interested. So it will probably be a long time before the Burma soil work is finished. This technique holds real possibilities for dating and might be applied to your work, Bill.

The other approach, which is just being started at the Department of Terrestrial Magnetism of the Carnegie Institution, is the change in orientation of iron-bearing particles in rocks and soils due to magnetic declination. This magnetic orientation varies with the change in position of magnetic north in different periods of time. They're just at the start of getting information. As I understand it, it's a very ticklish job; you must accurately place your samples of rock and soil in their original orientation before the measurements are made. Both of these techniques hold some hope for archaeological dating, but not this year.

GRIFFIN: I think that Johnson's fishweir study[14] is an excellent example of this ability to collaborate in fields of knowledge, which, to many individuals, are known only through coming across them casually in college catalogues. That impressive array of specialists is an example of the degree of sophistication in archaeological research, at least among some present-day archaeologists, over that displayed in the studies that were made on the fishweir when it was

[13]Krynine, 1939.   [14]Johnson *et al*, 1842, 1949.

first discovered. One of the major points of this particular seminar is, I think, not that archaeologists should become specialists in all these fields which might be applicable, but that they should have cognizance of the fact that such studies would be of extreme importance to them in archaeology and that they should enlist individuals in other fields to collaborate with them. Also, it provides other scientists with a great deal of new information which they have not had and which they can integrate into their own studies, so that normally, I think, a man whose imagination becomes fired by this type of collaboration will gain at least as much from it as the archaeologist will.

JOHNSON: Collaboration works both ways. It isn't collaboration, nor is it of any service unless it does.

GRIFFIN: I use your report in a course in North American archaeology to read to the class the names of the specialties of these individuals, and I hold up the volume to indicate the size and say that this section is what the archaeologist wrote and the rest is by men in these other fields.

RITCHIE: In the matter of the collaboration of the archaeologist with these specialists, there is a further point which might be pertinent to this discussion, namely, what the former's excavations in middens and village sites can provide for the zoologist. For instance, right now the zoologist of the State Science Service of New York is engaged on the problem of when the Virginia deer first entered the New England area. The frequency of the remains of the various species and the possible changes in the dentition of animals through a considerable period of time are among the valuable zoological data which can be provided by the archaeologist.

JOHNSON: Glover Allen, of the Museum of Comparative Zoology at Cambridge, worked on a similar problem which was concerned with the migrations of the gray seal up and down the coast. I don't think it had been published at the time of his death.

COLLIER: The history of corn, which is of great interest to some botanists, is very dependent on archaeological evidence. That makes me think of a point which bears on your remark that an archaeologist should not expect to get too much information from sending samples to a specialist with a few notes on how they were found. I'm thinking of the case of the plant materials collected by Junius Bird at Huaca Prieta.[15] A large part of those are being studied at Chicago by Cutler, a botanist with a special interest in the history of some of the cultivated plants of the Indians. Fortunately, Junius made quite an extensive collection of the present-day wild plants growing in that part of Peru. Cutler has remarked to me that this botanical collection is very useful to him, that he can get a great deal more out of the material than he has obtained from comparable lots that are simply specimens dug out of a site with notes on the level and nothing else. This is one small example of the very great extension of knowledge that can come from the gathering of some additional field data, either by the specialist or, in some cases, by the archaeologist, one who knows something about the problem and is interested in it. It adds tremendously to the knowledge and information that can be gotten out of archaeological specimens.

BREW: I would like to add a confirmation of that. In the ethnobotanical work at Awatovi, which was done by Volney Jones of the University of Michigan, Jones worked on the material which we were excavating. At the same time, his wife, who is also a botanist, endeavored to collect samples of every plant now growing in the vicinity. Unless you know that the specialist who is going to do the analysis of your plant material already has a full collection from the area concerned, a check of this sort is necessary.

COLLIER: There are very few places where that's true. Almost always there's something.

JOHNSON: We did the same thing at Grassy Island.[16] We made a collection of plants growing around the beach before we even started to dig. Furthermore, collections were made in the spring, in the midsummer, and in the late fall in order to get the differences in vegetation at different times of the year. The purpose of this was to provide a background for a projected pollen analysis of the deposits.

---

[15]Bird, 1948.   [16]Johnson and Raup, 1947.

Recent Developments in the Treatment of Archaeological Textiles

Junius Bird

This topic is of limited interest to most American archaeologists for the simple reason that prehistoric textiles are encountered in only a few areas. In those areas, however, particularly in the coastal deserts of Peru and Chile, the amount of such material which can be collected is far greater than is generally realized. Until recently, the major source of ancient textiles has been the tombs and burials opened by professional collectors whose only criterion for selection of textiles has been whether or not a piece or a section of one could be sold. Insofar as Peru is concerned, this resulted in a completely erroneous impression of the material available. For example, in 1945 I was assured that the prospects of finding fabrics of the Cupisnique-Chavin period were extremely unfavorable, only three or four oxidized scraps having been recovered from the many graves of that period which had been opened. Actually, I believe that in three months with a ten-man crew a collection of 2000 to 3000 fabrics of that period could be gathered. This seems reasonable in view of the large number of still older fabrics recently collected—some of them perhaps twice as old as the Cupisnique specimens.

This productive source is not the graves but the midden debris. Not until the establishment of the Andean Institute projects in Peru and Chile in 1941 were stratigraphic series of textiles collected from the middens. These projects and subsequent work have indicated the potential yield one can expect from certain sites. Of course, such textiles do not have the beauty and appeal of the best of the fabrics from the tombs, but they do provide a truer picture of the material in common use. They also give a surprising range of information about the people who made them, probably more than can be derived from any other of the commonly associated artifacts. From the fibers alone a fairly valid conclusion can be reached as to whether wild or domesticated plants and animals were the source. From the dyes or lack of dyes and mordants can be gauged the degree of applied chemistry of a culture. From such a simple thing as the direction of twist in spinning one may deduce broad regional relationship. From certain features of construction it is possible to show where mathematical calculations are involved. By judging the execution of such features one can even hazard an estimate of the personality of the weavers. The quality of the spinning and weaving furnishes a gauge of technological achievement, and where designs or patterns are used the possible deductions increase. Incidentally, I think the designs of textiles are more useful for long-range comparisons than are those on pottery. If there is any feeling that such comments as the preceding are afield from the topic of this paper, it should be remembered that most Peruvianists have neglected the prehistoric textile resources. It is my conviction that this will be an increasingly valuable field of research. Interest in it should be stimulated and knowledge of how to collect and properly handle fabrics should be developed.

It is not my purpose to tell you how to clean old textiles, but rather to call to your attention what has been accomplished and what can be done. The inspiration for this comes primarily from the Textile Museum in Washington, D.C., where, at the invitation of Mr. George H. Myers, a two-day conference on textile "cleaning" was held on January 17 and 18, 1949. This dealt with the work of Miss Louisa Bellinger and Mrs. Francina Greene and was not limited to cleaning, but covered analysis, fiber identification, mounting, and storage. It resulted in a projected series of short publications, <u>Workshop Notes</u>, the first issue of which deals with wool textiles.[17] Similar reports on textiles of other fibers are in preparation. This is a big step forward, for a few years ago the only published advice one could find on the treatment of old textiles was that one should mount them on a good quality of linen!

In reviewing the present status of the problem I must confess that I have little to suggest in the way of field techniques. If textiles are present in any quantity they can generally be packed in bulk with little risk of damage. Badly decomposed or oxidized pieces are better studied in the field, but where this is impractical pieces can be successfully shipped by packing them in the dust of the more completely decomposed parts of the same specimen. Hardening procedures using dilute shellac, ambroid, or alvar should be

---

[17]Greene, n.d.

employed with caution and should be fully understood. It is possible in some instances to reinforce a partly rotted fabric with rice paper and shellac as it is uncovered, but my experience with this procedure has not been satisfactory. The subsequent cleaning and mounting of the better preserved areas is made more difficult, and the bady rotted sections so treated are of slight value.

Another procedure has been suggested for small, extremely delicate pieces; they may be cemented to glass. The process, described in American Antiquity,[18] can be used in either field or laboratory when the specimens are of sufficient rarity to justify the work involved. If the recommended coating for the glass dries too rapidly, it should be remembered that the use of amyl acetate with acetone retards the drying. Perhaps the most important suggestion I can make for field procedure does not relate to the treatment but is simply the caution that no arbitrary selection or sampling and discarding should be made from material in stratified sites. Ideally, this might always be the case, but if one is dealing with looted cemeteries where the yield may be so bulky as to prevent shipment of all the material found he should at least save sections showing loom width of what seem to be nothing more than undecorated plain fabric fragments.

Back at the museum one must make certain basic decisions. If a large collection is involved, he must decide if the cleaning is to achieve maximum results as far as general appearance goes with probably some damage to fibers, or if the cleaning should stop short of injury to fibers in order to have the piece in best possible condition for analytical study. Most museums cannot afford to process a large series with the same care and effort which a rare item might receive, and thus a compromise may be necessary.

For the treatment of the more valuable or important specimens, I believe that the Textile Museum has the best advice, in part already published. In brief, this follows certain steps: identification of the fibers, note of spinning direction, and tests for dye fastness. Differences in these call for different procedures, all of which, however, require keeping the specimen between screening during different stages of the cleaning process. This eliminates stress from folding and handling, and its importance cannot be overemphasized. Whether a plastic or a wire screen with cheesecloth padding is used makes little difference.

[18] Laudermilk, 1937.

When, however, a great lot of specimens must be processed some more practical method is indicated, and at this time tests are being made to see what procedure is most suitable.

In my own work, which the Viking Fund generously aided, we were dealing with a quantity of salt-impregnated dirt-encrusted pieces of varying degrees of preservation. The majority are of cotton with bast plied with cotton in some instances. None are of wool. Color contrasts depend primarily on the use of natural shades of cotton; dye appears to be limited to blue and is of infrequent occurrence, while the use of a powdery red pigment is more common. Some of these fabrics are so badly rotted that it is probably just the salt impregnation that really holds them together and enables one to handle them at all. As it also binds the dirt to the yarns, the first step in cleaning is to remove the salt. Merely placing them in water might cause almost entire disintegration and so a method is called for that will protect the specimens while soaking and yet allow the salt to be dissolved. The methods used at the Textile Museum would have yielded good results, but the expense of so handling several thousand specimens was prohibitive. As an alternative, the following procedure was tried with sufficiently good results to warrant putting on record.

First, the textiles, taken as they were found in salt-encrusted wads, were sacked several at a time in cheesecloth and dipped in a solution made of one part commercial ambroid cement to nine parts acetone. When thoroughly saturated the specimens were spread on wire screening to dry with no attempt made to unfold them. The colodin strengthens the weaker areas and items sufficiently so that they can be repackaged in cheesecloth and soaked in water for two to three days without damage while the salt dissolves. This, however, does little cleaning, although some coarser lumps of dirt may loosen. After the excess water was drained off the specimens, still in the same cheesecloth bags, were placed in jars of acetone, which dehydrates and later softens the ambroid. By shifting the packages through a succession of jars of acetone the ambroid and ultimately most of the dirt can be removed by agitating the packages. For the particular problem involved with this large collection, the treatment resulted in a minimum amount of damage. At the Textile Museum specimens while still wet are spread out on plastic screening. I find, however, that there is less strain on the fibers if they are unfolded after they have been removed from the acetone and placed on a piece of composition board like "celotex" or "homosote" covered with a paper surfaced with aluminum foil. Pins will penetrate the board, and the smooth nonabsorbent surface of the foil prevents friction on even the most delicate sections which might otherwise pull away and tear. At this stage the yarns should be arranged as nearly as possible in their original directions.

Further cleaning, following the Textile Museum procedure, can be done in specific cases in which some dirt remains or if the specimen is of sufficient interest to warrant the effort. Having dried flat after the acetone bath they can be easily placed between screens, then sponge-washed with detergents or soap, and soft brush tamping may be applied where needed. When the fibers have lost original resiliency and cannot be mechanically loosened as they dry after a water bath, the yarns tend to collapse and mat. This can to some extent be avoided by final dehydration in acetone, or the dry piece can be saturated with benzene, and while this evaporates an artist's small jet airbrush with the pressure adjusted to about thirty-five pounds will loosen the fibers without damage.

These few comments deal almost exclusively with the specific problem posed by one large lot of very old, salt-encrusted fabrics of considerable interest and importance. It is not a method which can be recommended for materials in bulk, such as have been and will be collected from the Peruvian cemeteries. Much of this retains surprising strength, and probably could be sacked in netted bags, machine-washed, and spun-dried. I would suggest, however, that before such a procedure is attempted the Textile Museum staff be consulted. [19]

Slides Shown

1. An uncleaned fragment of basketry combining two types of material, cotton yarns heavily caked with dirt passing around strands of a sedge which are extremely brittle. By first hardening such a piece it can be freed of salt and dirt without damage to the sedge. As a final step after cleaning it should be strengthened with a thin colodin solution.

---

[19] For further information on preservation of textiles, see Sylwan, 1941, 1949.

2. A twined cotton fabric as it came from the ground showing an angular break, the result of bending the specimen while still impregnated with salt.

3, 4. A twined cotton fabric with some blue dye in the end weft after cleaning.

5, 6, 7, 8. Examples of cotton fabrics of various types after cleaning.

DISCUSSION

JOHNSON: Is that curly appearance of the fibers attributable to wear?

BIRD: Yes, it is due to erosion of the yarn. The same curly fiber ends are present even on specimens which have not been processed.

JOHNSON: When the yarn was new, did it have the same appearance?

BIRD: Not quite so much, but most of these fabrics are made of slack-spun yarns. It is an irregular yarn, and yarn hanks that have never been used show the same tendency to be fuzzy.

After one has cleaned the specimens and made an analysis of their structure, there remains the problem of how to store them. Folding them in "Lumarith" seems to be practical and not too expensive a method. In this they can be handled, and as study specimens they can be stored away in about as small an area as possible. We did check on the available plastics for covering them in storage and found that certain of the cellophanes as they break down in the course of years give off a gas which can damage the enclosed material. I believe the information came from the National Library in Washington. Some of their documents were damaged by storing them in the wrong type of cellophane. After various tests, it was found that this particular brand, known as "Lumarith," is suitable, and they believe it will not damage the specimens stored in it. Lumarith is put out by the Celanese Corporation. I believe some other firms put out the same type of plastic, but I don't know the brand names.

ORCHARD: I'd like to ask one question. You spoke of the

use of various types of acetates, such as ambroid. How much of those materials do you keep in the textiles permanently after you've accomplished the stiffening so that they can be handled?

BIRD: One leaves the acetate in just for the soaking stage, which may take three days. Incidentally, in soaking we find that sometimes it's advantageous to use a wetting agent like aeresol to increase the rate of penetration. The dust sometimes prevents the water from penetrating. I do not understand the reason, but I have seen dust-caked wadded textiles which, after three or four days in water, were still dry in part if no wetting agent had been used.

ORCHARD: My question was this: After you have soaked out the salt crystals, is the fabric still coated with the ambroid?

BIRD: Yes. This coating then dissolves in the acetone, which also lets the dirt fall out. I must repeat that this is not a cure-all for all prehistoric textiles. It was suitable for the particular problem we were faced with, and would probably not be needed for later material with more tensile strength. A few tests, comparing the strength of individual fibers that have been processed with ones that have not, showed that the processed ones are somewhat higher in strength. Why that should be I don't know, unless there is salt actually within the fibers giving them a tendency to break at some point where a very microscopic crystal of salt has formed.

RITCHIE: Do you have any other recommendations for the preservation of carbonized textiles, fragments of which we occasionally find in our area?

BIRD: The pasting of the fragment between two pieces of glass with a filler so that the glass doesn't press against the specimen might conceivably work, although I have not used this system.

BREW: Of course, this entire business of carbonized textiles, which is the condition in which we usually get them in the open sites of North America, illustrates the difference in process very nicely, because in that case you have to treat them in the field before you take them out of the ground. What we did at Awatovi was very simple first-aid business— by very carefully introducing a piece of cardboard, usually something torn off a carton, underneath the fragment, then carefully putting the alvar solution over it, we had the whole textile. But, of course, that's an entirely different problem from yours.

BIRD: We have also tried embedding textiles in a clear plastic, methyl methacrylate, with good results. Colors appear slightly altered as though the fabric were wet. The best application of this method is probably for small pieces in which the fibers have lost their tensile strength, and the specimen cannot be handled for study. At present, it is not feasible to do this work in the field.

SPAULDING: I have heard that alvar in alcohol was a good general agent to use in the field for that purpose.

BIRD: No, I have never tried that.

JOHNSON: We have used alvar in alcohol. In the Southeast, you sometimes have to work with materials that are damp. Alvar in acetone makes a white skin over the specimen which does not expel the water and is not strong. By using alcohol to dehydrate the specimen and the ground around it, and then by treating it with alvar in alcohol, you can sometimes save a specimen.

GRIFFIN: Where have you been able to have your textiles identified?

BIRD: A series of cotton fibers from this collection was checked by J. B. Hutchinson, S. G. Stephens, and S. C. Harland at the Shirley Institute at Manchester, England. Dr. A. C. Whitford is perhaps the best authority on the cameloid wools from South America and has also worked with the native fibers of North America.[20]

The identification of fibers, particularly the basts, requires considerable experience. If a series of properly identified fibers mounted on microscope slides were available, it would simplify the problem.

[20] Whitford, 1941.

Principles in the Conservation of Mural Paintings

Rutherford J. Gettens

In the preservation of historic buildings and ruins and in the salvage of archaeological finds the problem of the conservation of mural paintings is not often encountered. When this problem arises, however, it is apt to be difficult. There are no established routine procedures as there are for the treatment of easel paintings. Field archaeologists usually have had no previous experience, and the literature on the subject is sparse. Mural paintings, moreover, are usually attached and are part of the site or else they are large and unwieldy and impossible to transport to a convenient workshop. Sometimes the task of preservation is judged impracticable or even impossible, and in that event an artist is called upon to make copies or reproductions, after which the paintings are abandoned. On the other hand, it is sometimes felt that every effort must be made to preserve the paintings and to save them from the elements or from despoilers, or it is thought that because of their historical significance they should be taken from a remote and little-seen location to a place where they can be made more accessible to the public. When such operations are required, there are seldom specialists at hand. The archaeologist must do the best he can, usually with limited resources. Some field operations have been wonderfully successful, but other attempts at recovery have been disappointing or even dismal failures. It is the purpose of this paper to analyze the problem of mural painting conservation, to outline methods of treatment, to point out faulty practices, and to state the principles of a seemingly rational practice which has been developed from the experience of several workers in the Fogg Museum over a period of years. Time, however, does not permit me to go into all the details of wall-painting treatment. Each job frequently turns out to be a special problem, hence some experimentation is usually required in respect to the problem at hand, whether it is an entire wall painting in situ or one brought to the laboratory in several sections. It is an advantage before proceeding with a conservation job to determine the materials and structure of the painting through careful preliminary examination.

I. TYPES OF MURAL PAINTINGS

Mural paintings are pictorial representations which are fixed to walls of buildings, sides of cliffs, or interiors of caves. The ancient and primitive ones were usually painted thinly with aqueous mediums on porous surfaces. Mediums ranged from animal glue to vegetable gums.[21] The most distinguishing feature is perhaps the kind of support. A classification based on type of support is as follows:

1. Rock or masonry
   The paintings may have been applied directly to the stone or over a thin priming. Examples: interiors of the rock-hewn temples of China; paintings on block limestone walls in Egypt and Yucatan.

2. Lime-sand plaster on masonry, stucco, or adobe walls
   a) Painted in true fresco (painting in wet plaster without organic binder). Example: Renaissance wall paintings in Italy.
   b) Painted in secco (painting in tempera on dry plaster walls). Example: Renaissance wall paintings in Italy.

3. Neat lime plaster on masonry, stucco, or adobe walls
   Examples: mural paintings of the Aegean Age in Crete and the paintings recently discovered on the walls of the Maya temple at Bonampak in southern Mexico.

4. Gypsum plaster
   a) Solid gypsum plaster. Examples: Roman mural paintings found at Dura Europas in Syria and also many Egyptian mural paintings.
   b) Gypsum coating on lime-sand plaster. Example: interior walls of some of the Spanish mission churches of the American Southwest.

---

[21]Mural paintings, even from earliest times, were done also in other mediums and techniques, such as encaustic, fresco, and oil, but even when these more specialized mediums were used the problem of conservation is essentially the same.

CONSERVATION OF MURAL PAINTINGS

5. Mud or clay walls
   a) With fibrous binder, like straw or hair, and usually finished with a priming of kaolin. Example: temple paintings of China and Japan.
   b) Without fibrous binder and usually finished with a coating of fine clay. Example: prehistoric kiva paintings of the American Southwest.

Deterioration and methods of treatment of all these classes of wall paintings are similar. Since, however, the last class, the mud-wall type of painting, is of chief interest to American archaeologists, this discussion is directed chiefly to that class.

II. DETERIORATION OF MURAL PAINTINGS

The kinds of defects that mural paintings acquire with age and neglect are numerous. They range from dust accretions to holes and losses caused by acts of vandalism. It is possible roughly to classify defects:

First, there are structural insecurities of walls caused by weakening of the foundation, loss of roof, decay of support timbers, vegetation, and wind and water erosion.

Second, there are structural insecurities of superimposed layers caused by cleavage and weakness of material. Cleavage results from poor adhesion or insufficient bond between differently composed layers. It is serious when it is caused by breaking of the keys that bond plaster walls to masonry; because of excessive weight large areas may fall and become permanently lost. When cleavage occurs between layers of mud or plaster the same is true, but to a lesser degree. Here it may be caused by moisture conditions, by roots from vegetable matter, and by structural faults. When cleavage exists between the paint film and the wall it results in scaling. Cleavage in paint films made from aqueous paints, however, is ordinarily not frequent or serious. That is more commonly the defect of medium-rich films. Weakness of material is perhaps a more common defect. Except in the fiber-bonded wall paintings of China, mud walls are apt to be crumbly and friable. Repeated recrystallization of soluble salts within the wall structure, caused by alternate wet and dry conditions, can completely destroy walls and paintings. Organic binders in paint layers can become ineffective from bacterial decomposition. When structures and films suffer from body weakness, loss is usually from abrasion, not from cleavage.

The third and perhaps most disturbing kind of defect is disfigurement of the design because the design is that part which is of chief interest. It may be harmed in many ways, principally by stains and accretions from dripping water, wind-blown dust, smoke and soot, and bird droppings. The design may suffer through loss of paint by scaling and abrasion. Optical defects caused by fading of color and chalking of the surface may make the design difficult to read.

III. PRINCIPLES OF TREATMENT

We may now consider the different phases of treatment in the same sequence in which we discussed deterioration and defects, since in actual practice they would be taken up in that order. Correction of structural insecurities of the walls may be the first necessary step if it is desired to leave the wall paintings in place and to treat them in situ. Circumstances and conditions will vary greatly from site to site, and methods of treatment will depend largely on local requirements and facilities. Wall stabilization is often a semiengineering problem. Archaeologists of the National Park Service have lately been engaged in this task, and it is understood that they have worked out some satisfactory techniques. Discussion of those stabilization practices is, however, outside the scope of this paper.

It often happens that the walls are beyond repair or strengthening, and thus it is necessary to attempt to separate the painting from the walls and let the walls go. Or it may happen that the walls are in good enough condition but the painting is in a remote locality; consequently, it is desired to move the painting to a cultural center where it will be accessible to many. If removal is necessary, the following courses of action are open:

If the walls are not engaged to rock or masonry or especially if they are interior walls with a hollow or space in the back, they may be cut into sections, supported in frames or in shallow boxes with a suitable packing material, and shipped long distances. Most of the large Chinese wall paintings that have been brought to this country by dealers were handled in that way. Some have been cut into thirty or more sections with individual pieces as large as four by five feet square. Such removed sections have been mounted in Portland cement or backed with iron-re-enforced plaster of Paris. There is always the problem of getting such heavy and unwieldy sections reassembled so that each piece is supported independently and in proper register. A number of large Oriental wall paintings have been treated in this way with good results but presumably at excessive cost.[22] Often, however, this type of mounting is too heavy and cumbersome or the wall support itself is too fragile and crumbly to justify removal or salvage. In that case a second course of action is possible; that is to separate the design layer entirely from its original wall and transfer it to a new and more manageable support. Although transfer of paintings ordinarily requires no small amount of skill and training, yet transfer operations have been carried out successfully under field conditions by operators who have had little previous experience.

There are two principal methods of transfer:[23]

The first is the "back removal" method which is applicable to disengaged walls or sections of walls. The process briefly is this: The surface of the wall is impregnated or fixed with a water-insoluble colorless lacquer. After this has dried a paper and cloth facing is applied with a plasticized water-soluble glue. When the facing is set, the section is turned face down and all excess clay and mud support removed from the back right down to the reverse side of the paint film. A fabric re-enforcement is attached to the reverse, and then the section is mounted with the back down on a building board or other support with synthetic resin adhesive. After drying for some days the facing is soaked away from the front to reveal the original face side of the painting. As an alternative, which might offer advantages under certain circumstances, the facing may be applied with the same plastic adhesive used to fix the paint surface, but

---

[22]In several museums in this country, notably in the University of Pennsylvania Museum in Philadelphia, at the William Rockhill Nelson Gallery of Art in Kansas City, and at the Cranbrook Museum in Bloomfield Hills, Michigan, one can see examples of colossal Buddhist wall paintings from China which were cut up into large rectangular sections and later backed in this way. It appears that this kind of mounting was mostly done in Paris, France, for the dealer Mr. C. T. Loo.

[23]These methods of transfer are no new discovery. They were developed in Italy, in the eighteenth century.

when that is done an organic-solvent insoluble adhesive, such as animal glue, must be used to attach the back of the transfer to the new support. There must be a solvent differential between the facing adhesive and the adhesive to the permanent support to allow removal of the facing after remounting. Several large Chinese mural paintings have been treated in this way with quite good results.[24] During the transfer process cleaning of the surface and repair of breaks in the surface can be made.

The second means which may be called the "front removal" method of transfer is employed when it is not possible to get at the back of the wall or to cut it up for convenient handling in the workshop. It is a stripping or pulling technique which can be applied when the painting must be taken from the wall in situ. As in the back removal method a paper and cloth facing is applied to a marked-out section of the mural surface by use of a specially strong adhesive. When dry the facing is peeled off, and if the bond between the facing and the paint is stronger than the bond between paint and support, the paint is detached with the facing. After preparation of the reverse side of the paint film by removal of excess wall material the paint is smoothed down, and perhaps a thin fabric is attached. The section is then joined to its new support, either fabric or wallboard, and the facing is removed from the front as in the back removal method. This mode of transfer has been employed for the removal of Italian fresco paintings. Mr. Watson Smith, of the Peabody Museum, Harvard, used it successfully in recovering superimposed kiva paintings at Awatovi in Arizona.[25]

Both of these methods of transfer are ticklish and difficult operations and usually require experimentation and practice. There are many complicating factors that require skill in preparation and manipulation of materials and in the timing of operations. Transfer under field conditions may require quite different properties in materials and variations in procedures from those employed under laboratory conditions. I refer you to the literature for further details.

Insecurity of the superimposed layers between the design layer and the wall proper may also be sufficient justification

---

[24] Examples can be seen at the Museum of Fine Arts, Boston, the Philadelphia Museum of Art, and the Royal Ontario Museum of Art and Archaeology, Toronto, Canada.

[25] Smith, n.d.

for transfer. There are many instances, however, where
transfer is impractical or unjustifiable and accordingly the
walls must be treated in place. Cleavage between superimposed layers probably does not occur so much in mud-wall
paintings as it does in oil or tempera paintings because the
composition is usually more homogeneous. It may occur,
nevertheless, and when it does, it is always a difficult defect to handle. In case of local cleavage areas the old
practice was to force an adhesive, like glue, along broken
edges or through cracks or to squirt it in with a syringe.
Modern plastic adhesives and molten wax-resin mixtures can
also be used. Pressure is required, of course, during
setting. One is at a disadvantage in trying to carry out
such an operation on a vertical wall. When the entire layered
structure has become disintegrated from internal salt recrystallization or from other causes there is little one can do
except try to remove the agencies of decay. It is possible
to coat surfaces with plastic bonding agents and to force them
into the interior by flooding the surface with organic solvents.
Care must be taken, however, to get deep penetration and not
to create a skin effect at the surface.

The last major step is usually treatment of disfigurement
of the design. There can be, however, no rules or standard
practice for removal of stains and accretions. Some will
brush off easily while others will be resistant and difficult. If
the painting is transferred, cleaning is ordinarily done during
or after removal of the facing because at that time the surface is not so tender since it is protected by the fixing coat.
Often much cleaning has to be accomplished by mechanical
means. If the painting is to be cleaned *in situ*, cleaning is
usually done after the wall surface has been consolidated or
fixed with a spray. If there are extensive areas of paint
loss, they may have to be filled in at least partly to make
the design readable. In addition to losses of paint by scaling
there may be deep holes, bare patches, and fissures. These
will require filling up to the level of the paint surface to prevent further losses at the edges. Often a luting made from
powdered wall material and plastic binder will serve. If the
paint losses are small the area of loss may be painted in
with a closely similar tone so that the composition will not
be disfigured. If areas of loss are extensive, major elements
of the design may have to be connected to pull the composition together. In an otherwise unharmed mural, dust and
chalking of the surface may have caused lowering of tones and

dimming of contrasts. If a lacquer has not already been used in the facing process, these optical defects may be corrected with a thin plastic spray, care being taken not to give the surface an undesirable gloss.

In summary, the whole purpose of treatment is to effect consolidation and strengthening of the support for the design layer and to make secure its attachment to the support. At the same time it is necessary to avoid changing the texture and character of the surface, which can result from the use of excess fixative and adhesive. Care should be taken not to employ materials and techniques that give temporarily satisfactory results, but which eventually hasten the destruction of the design. Unfortunately, there have been instances where that has happened.

IV. MATERIALS OF TREATMENT

All these manipulations described require the use of adhesives, fixatives, binders, and coatings, the choice of which may be the key to success or the cause of failure. It is about these that most questions are asked and also it is about these that there is most misunderstanding. Most adhesive and coating materials are organic in composition, and unfortunately they all have a tendency, as time goes on, to yellow, to get harder and more brittle, and to shrink and contract. Some become immediately insoluble; others become that way with time. The useful life of these materials may be much shorter than that of the original materials of the wall paintings. If they are applied in excess either as adhesives or as coatings, they may create stresses in the interior or case hardening at the surface. Plasticizers are often combined with organic film-forming materials to make flexible coatings, but plasticizers themselves slowly evaporate or lose their effect.

Coating and adhesive materials for wall-painting treatment should, in general, come as close as possible to satisfying the following ideal requirements: (1) They should be colorless or nearly colorless when applied and should not yellow or change color with age. (2) They should remain permanently plastic and flexible. (3) For compounding purposes they should be readily soluble in solvents so that they will not be too viscous in low concentrations and will penetrate easily and evenly into porous surfaces. (4) They should be soluble in solvents that are not too volatile to facilitate penetration. (5) They should form films that can be redissolved, if necessary.

No single material, of course, satisfies all of these requirements. In our own experience, however, especially in the conservation of Oriental wall paintings, we have found a few classes of materials which come nearest to satisfying the above specifications. These are:

Synthetic polymers of vinyl acetate, vinyl acetal, methyl and butyl methacrylate and related compounds. These are sold under a variety of trade names and may be purchased in solid form or in solution.[26] They form colorless or nearly colorless films, they dissolve readily in a variety of solvents, and they make good adhesives. Like all polymers they get brittle with age and decrease in solubility, but in this respect they are rather better than many other synthetics sometimes employed for the same purposes. It is possible for the amateur to compound small batches of these synthetics, but when large batches are required or special properties are desired it is better to turn the job over to a paint or lacquer laboratory.

Waxes. These include paraffin, beeswax, carnauba, and synthetic waxes. Their main feature is a low melting point which allows them to be applied in the molten state; on cooling they set rapidly. In special cases waxes may be used for setting cleavage where a strong adhesive is not necessary. Waxes in solution may be used for coatings, but on mural paintings they are generally not serviceable because they modify too much the visual character of the surface. Waxes, however, change little with age, and they are permanently soluble. Soft resins may be added to waxes to increase their adhesiveness and hardness, but if used in too great proportion they will impart to the wax all the defects inherent in soft natural resins, such as yellowing and embrittlement.

Animal glue or gelatin. A good grade of gelatin will form a film that is nearly colorless and will not yellow with age.

---

[26] Vinyl acetate in different viscosities may be purchased from the Bakelite Corporation of America; vinyl acetal is supplied by the Shawinigan Chemical Corporation, Empire State Building, New York City. Methacrylate resins are obtainable from E. I. DuPont de Nemours and Co., of Wilmington, Delaware. All these companies supply data sheets which give the properties and uses of these compounds.

Dried gelatin serves as a tough, strong adhesive even when employed in low concentrations and in minimum amounts. Many examples of five-centuries-old Italian gesso (gypsum with glue binder) have been seen which are still strong and tough, even though the glue content is only 5 to 10 per cent by weight. Gelatin in thin solution is good for setting cleavage and for consolidating weakened layers. The films are completely insoluble in organic solvents, a quality which makes them useful in transfer operations where preferential solubilities are necessary. They are permanently soluble in water, which may or may not be an advantage depending upon circumstances. Although gelatin is a protein and readily suffers bacterial decomposition when damp, yet there are instances where gelatin films have existed for centuries, even millenniums, without apparent change. There are now available good fungicides, such as the phenyl mercurials, which can lessen this defect.

It is impossible to go into details here concerning formulation and application of these materials. Some of that detail may be found, however, in the rather meager literature on this subject.[27]

Unfortunately, there have been employed in the past for treatment of mural paintings certain materials which, in the light of our own experience, are not generally suitable for that purpose. Among these are:

Casein. This milk product, which is used generally as an adhesive, forms hard brittle films which are permanently insoluble. When used in excess it causes shrinkage, crackle, and cleavage. It yellows and, because it is a protein, it suffers bacterial decomposition if allowed to remain in a damp environment.

Cellulose plastics: nitrocellulose, cellulose acetate, and others. These compounds are viscous in low concentrations in organic solvents, even when strong solvents are employed. Cellulosic coatings do not penetrate well, but form skins at the surface which crack and peel and discolor with time. Nitrocellulose (pyroxylin, Celluloid, and guncotton) in particular is not a permanently stable substance.

---

[27] See Anon., Bliss, Coremans, Forni, Gettens, Lavagnino, Smith, Stopelaëre, Stout, Stout and Gettens, Suardo, and White in Selected Bibliography.

Shellac. Even bleached shellac is seldom desirable. It produces hazy films which, when yellowed, permanently lower the tone quality of the surface, and the films become less soluble with age and difficult to remove.

In conservation of mural paintings choice of materials is important, but even more important is the way in which they are used. Properly used inferior materials can sometimes do a better job than improperly used good ones. Perhaps the most important single principle to be observed in the use of coatings and adhesives is that they should be used in the minimum amount required for a purpose and no more. That amount which is in excess will probably do more harm than good. Conservation, like the culinary art, is perhaps nine-tenths technique and one-tenth science.

DISCUSSION

FEJOS: I would like to ask whether there is any definite difference between fresco and secco murals. Would you be able to point out the difference or would it be too long a discussion?

GETTENS: Buon fresco is the Italian term used to describe painting done on a wet lime-plaster wall without use of an organic binder. The pigment is locked in at the surface by the setting of the lime and becomes part of the wall itself. Secco, as its name indicates, describes painting done on a dry lime-plaster wall with a water-thinned medium like egg or glue. Since the paint film is not an integral part of the wall it can separate and scale from the plaster. It is often difficult to distinguish secco painting from fresco, especially if the former is applied thinly. The term "secco" has often been used to describe any type of water paint applied to a dry surface, as in the primitive paintings of the Southwest, or the glue-tempera paintings of the Far East. Paint films applied heavily by the secco technique seem to have a greater tendency to abrade and cleave from the plaster support and hence offer a greater problem in conservation.

BREW: I am not prepared to discuss the technical aspects of mural painting. I can say, however, that we had a really mean job at Awatovi where we had the paintings superimposed, so that we quite normally were dealing with walls with forty to fifty layers of plaster, sometimes plain plaster, many of them painted. In one case, we ran up as high as over two hundred layers. The problem there was to peel off one layer with the painting on without destroying the ones underneath. With the technique Mr. Watson Smith worked out, based on Mr. Getten's advice, we succeeded in doing this successfully. I don't suppose you have his book on your list. The publication is now in press and will be out sometime within the next two or three years, depending on how long it takes us to get satisfactory color plates.[28]

BRAINERD: What about the comparative usefulness of alvar and ambroid techniques?

GETTENS: Alvar is the trade name for polyvinylacetal, which I mentioned. It is similar to polyvinylacetate, and, in my opinion, is a fairly good material because it's so readily soluble in many solvents. You get deep penetration and good distribution. We have never used ambroid, because we believe that it is essentially a cellulose nitrate compound. It is much too dark in color to be used near the surface of a painting.

BREW: They also make it white, although the white is not really white.

GETTENS: If it is a cellulose nitrate material, I wouldn't care to use it. I don't think nitrate films have a very long life; they usually have to be loaded with plasticizer and the plasticizer eventually disappears.

BREW: Is dibutyl phthalate a plasticizer?

GETTENS: Yes.

BREW: We used that on the Awatovi kiva paintings which were taken out from 1936 to 1939. We kept one small piece which we didn't mount in the museum, and it's still in perfectly plastic shape — you can roll it up. It works very nicely.

---

[28]Smith, n.d.

GETTENS: That's doing unusually well, I should say.

BREW: I took it out last week to show to someone, and I wouldn't be prepared to say it was any stiffer. It probably is. It should be, of course.

BRAINERD: Do you ever use a substance, which is water soluble, called polyvinal alcohol?

GETTENS: Yes, we have used it as an adhesive to some extent, but we've never used it as a coating material. I don't think it gives very good, clear films; it isn't designed for that purpose. It is rather an interesting material. It has one advantage: like the other polyvinal compounds it does not seem to mildew or readily suffer bacterial decomposition. Polyvinal compounds are outstanding in that respect.

BRAINERD: I've used it in making gesso coatings and find very little shrinkage.

GETTENS: We haven't used polyvinal alcohol a great deal. Someone has said it should be the perfect water-color medium because it doen't seem to be subject to bacterial decomposition as gum arabic is.

BREW: The next paper is by S. F. Cook, who is professor of physiology at the University of California. He will talk to us on the subject "Chemical Analysis of Fossil Bone."[29]

COOK: The problem to be discussed is how may one determine by chemical analysis whether or not a human bone and an animal bone found in the same horizon were contemporaneous. In the Berkeley laboratory we have worked on two sets of samples. The first set consisted of a human bone and a horse bone from a cave in Calaveras County. The horse bones were undoubtedly late Pleistocene. We determined the values for water, nitrogen, organic carbon, and fluoride in both human and horse bone. The second set consisted of five human bones and five horse or camel bones from what is known as the Tranquility site[30] in Fresno County, which has been excavated recently by the University of Pennsylvania. For the

---

[29] See also Cook, 1951.   [30] Hewes, 1946.

Calaveras site the human bones gave us from two to fifty times as much water, nitrogen, and carbon as the horse bone, whereas the latter was far higher in fluoride than the former. From this result, we concluded that the human bones are very recent; the horse bones are unquestionably ancient. In other words, these specimens are in no way to be regarded as contemporaneous. In the case of the Tranquility site all four substances were found to be present in equal quantities in all the bones within experimental error. Since the mammal bones are definitely ancient—at least a good many thousand years old—we have concluded that the human remains are of approximately the same antiquity. With regard to relative age, it should be noted that the anthropologists at Berkeley, on the basis of artifacts found at the site, have placed the culture in the Middle period rather than the Early period in the Central Valley. With regard to absolute age, the problem still remains concerning the date of extinction of the Pleistocene fauna in California.

Chemical Analysis of Fossil Bone

Sherburne F. Cook

It has generally been assumed by archaeologists and paleontologists that when animal or human bone lies buried in the earth for long periods it undergoes a replacement by inorganic matter from the soil frequently referred to as "fossilization" or "mineralization." Few details concerning the mechanism of this change have been available. Recently, however, investigations along a number of parallel lines carried out jointly by the departments of physiology and anthropology of the University of California have shed new light on the problem. This report covers a part of the investigation as it stands at present.

The contribution of perhaps the most fundamental significance has been the electron micrographic study by one of our students, Mrs. Elizabeth P. Barbour.[31] She has been able to secure photographs of very thin bone fragments with a film magnification of 8000 diameters. Five samples have been studied: a femur of a laboratory rat, a normal human femur obtained from a cadaver, a human femur of relatively recent prehistoric time, perhaps 500 years old, from site CCo-138, a femur from a site of the early Central California culture period, SJo-142, and a femur from an ancient site on the south coast of California, LAn-1. All five showed a very characteristic structural pattern resembling a honeycomb with light spaces on the negatives surrounded by dark walls. The diameter of the light spaces ranged from 0.0062 to 0.0225 micron, whereas the bone cavities hitherto regarded as smallest, the canaliculae of the Haversian system, average 0.3 micron in diameter.

For reasons which are discussed in her paper Mrs. Barbour concluded that the discontinuous light spaces probably consist of organic matter together perhaps with water, whereas the continuous, dark, wall-like network is composed of inorganic compounds. The latter may be presumed to include primarily calcium phosphate and carbonate organized in some orderly structure.

[31]Barbour, 1950.

In a sense, the findings by means of the electron microscope technique merely sharpen and confirm the conclusion long since reached by investigators of bone who used purely chemical methods; bone consists of two clearly distinct types of compounds—inorganic, or mineral, and organic. The electron microscope data, however, clearly delimit the spatial relationship of the two primary components and make it very plain that in studying post-mortem changes the fate of the organic and inorganic materials may be very different and hence must be followed separately.

Calcium Phosphate and Calcium Carbonate

Apart from relatively small quantities of other elements and compounds the inorganic part of bone consists of phosphates and carbonates of calcium. The quantitative relationships of these substances in fossil bone have been studied during the past three years by two general methods: direct chemical analysis and a radioactive tracer technique.

Direct analyses have been carried out with groups of ten to thirty samples each from 17 Central California, 2 Southern California, and 4 Southwestern archaeological sites. In all instances the solid bone from the central part of the femur has been employed. The analyses included determinations of elementary calcium and phosphorus together with carbonate, as carbon dioxide. The procedures have been described in papers either published or in manuscript form.

When the average values of calcium for the 23 sites are inspected, there seems at first sight to be a significant increase of this element in the older bones. When the calcium values are correlated with those for the nonmineral fraction of the bones, however, there is a high negative coefficient. Conversely, a high positive coefficient characterizes the correlation between calcium and total content of inorganic matter. These relationships carry the strong implication that the fundamental change occurring as one passes from recent to old bone is a reduction in the organic matter and water with corresponding relative increase in the total inorganic fraction. Simultaneously, there appears to be very little alteration in the calcium content as such. This conclusion is made still more clear by taking the average calcium content of the 10 late sites, the 6 middle sites, and the 7 early sites. The values for the mean calcium content are, respectively, 35.13, 34.95, and 36.20 per cent. The small differences in the three figures possess no statistical or other significance.

Insofar as time as such is concerned, therefore, there is no alteration in the calcium content. For phosphorus the data support a similar conclusion.

With respect to carbon dioxide there is a slight increase in the older sites, the mean percentages for late, middle, and early sites being, respectively, 4.89, 6.30, and 7.02. It was this increase of CO_2 with duration of interment which led Professor Heizer and me to include the carbonate content as an entity which could be used as an index for the estimation of relative age. The extension of analyses from the Central Valley to include other geographical areas has made it clear, however, that such a tendency is not necessarily present and that the result given above is due principally to the heavy weighting given the Central Valley sites in the totals. It is likely that in the Sacramento Valley local soil conditions favored carbonate accumulation whereas the opposite might be true elsewhere. An outstanding instance of the reverse trend is seen at the Topanga site (LAn-1), known by cultural evidence to be very ancient. The bones from this locality contained even less carbon dioxide than may be found in the normal fresh human skeleton. For these reasons the relative carbonate content loses all universality as a criterion of age.

Although they cannot be systematically associated with age, it is apparent from analyses that the inorganic constituents of these long-buried bones have undergone some kind of alteration. Otherwise, the variation in calcium, phosphorus, and carbon dioxide content from site to site, in an apparently random manner, is capable of no reasonable explanation.

At this point it is worth while to re-examine the total inorganic content of the bones. When buried they contained, apart from organic material and water, primarily calcium phosphate and calcium carbonate. The small quantities of magnesium, chloride, fluoride, and so forth, which may have been present, would not affect the general situation. If at the present time the fossil bones retain the calcium salts in no very profoundly modified condition, and if no other changes have occurred, then the sum of the calcium phosphate and carbonate should still represent substantially the total inorganic fraction of the bone quite irrespective of any alteration in the organic fraction.

If, now, the calcium phosphate plus carbonate actually found by analysis is less than the total inorganic matter, then the difference must represent noncalcareous material which has been accumulated by the bone during its sojourn in the ground. If the calcium phosphate plus carbonate is equal to the total inorganic matter, then either no change has occurred or the bone has accumulated lime salts. If the phosphate plus carbonate is greater than the total observed inorganic matter, then we must invoke experimental error. As a matter of fact, the average difference for all the sites studied is a 5 per cent deficiency in the lime salts, indicating a general tendency for the bones to accumulate noncalcareous material.

On the other hand there are noteworthy differences among sites. For example, sites Sac-6, Sac-43, Sac-151, SJo-68, SJo-142, and Sac-107 all produce bones wherein the lime salts constitute nearly or quite all the inorganic fraction. This is an indication of little or no infiltration by foreign or noncalcareous substances, although it does not preclude the accumulation of the lime salts themselves. Now these six sites are all of a type which occurs frequently in the Central California Valley and which consists almost entirely of midden refuse with very little admixture of extraneous soil. Soil analyses have shown them to contain uniformly a high concentration of lime. Long periods of exposure to these high levels of calcium carbonate would very probably mean an infiltration of this material into the bone. Any such foreign or extrinsic carbonate would then be included in the laboratory analyses.

Sites CCo-141, Sac-104, Fre-48, and LAn-1 all produce bones in which the calcium phosphate and carbonate are definitely less than the total inorganic matter and hence must contain considerable noncalcareous material. Site CCo-141 lies in and is surrounded by an acid peat bog. The matrices of Sac-104 and Fre-48 consist predominantly of sandy alluvial deposits rather than undisturbed habitation middens. Site LAn-1 appears to contain an original mound deposit, but the latter is now altered to almost an adobe clay in which there are only faint traces of carbonate.

It is worth mentioning that the first group described produces bones which to visual inspection are compact, dense, white, and chalky, whereas the second group is characterized by light, porous, brown to black bones of almost woody consistency. Further evidence that one is here dealing with variation in the inorganic fraction is supplied by the electron micrographs of bones from Sac-107 and LAn-1. Although the basic geometrical pattern of each conforms to that found in fresh specimens, there are quantitative differences. Thus, the thickness of the honeycomb walls in the sample from Sac-107 is very much greater than in fresh bone, while that in the LAn-1 sample is much less. At the same time the carbonate content of the former (expressed as CO_2) is 10.8 per cent and of the latter 3 per cent.

From the results here presented the conclusion is warranted that changes take place in the inorganic component of bone during fossilization, but these changes are contingent in type and in direction upon the chemical nature of the soil or matrix in which the bones lie buried. No uniform and universal alteration merely with age can therefore be expected.

We have devoted considerable attention to the mechanism whereby such shifts in the mineral content of fossil bone may have been accomplished. It is possible to consider primarily the two acid radicals, phosphate and carbonate. Our detailed data show that although these components vary considerably from site to site and even from bone to bone, the primary positive element, calcium, is relatively constant. This implies that the total of the two anions fluctuates very little. That this is true is also implicit in the fact that the coefficient of variation for the sum of phosphate and carbonate is only one-fourth as large as that of the ratio of the two acid radicals.

An accumulation of either calcium carbonate or of noncalcareous material has been postulated as being conditioned by soil content. It is similarly possible that fluctuation in the relative quantities of carbonate and phosphate may also be referable to the substances forming the mound matrix, and furthermore that a loss as well as a gain may be incurred. This view has been tested by examination of the exchange of ions between the bone and an external solution.

That there is a continuous overturn of diffusible ions, particularly phosphate and carbonate, between the living bone and the blood plasma has long been appreciated, and considerable progress has been made in the study of the dynamics of the process. The physical and chemical conditions, however, are very dissimilar when the completely dead bone lies surrounded by soil. Hence our knowledge of the reactions proceeding during life cannot be carried over directly to the nonliving state. For present purposes, indeed, it should be sufficient to show that exchange of ions, specifically anions, can occur and does occur, without attempting to elucidate the kinetics of the reactions or to measure the equilibria involved. In an attempt to secure a direct answer to this question experiments were performed with fossil bone by the use of radioactive tracers and the standard counting technique.

Owing to the exigencies of space and time, these experiments cannot be discussed in detail at this point. A reasonably full description has been prepared, however, and will be available on request. Briefly, it could be shown that both phosphate and carbonate enter and leave fossil bone with relative ease and rapidity. It was also evident that the quantity thus involved is contingent on the state of subdivision of the bone and the type and concentration of the anions present in the external solution. It is legitimate to conclude from the data that the movement of phosphate and carbonate is based upon an interchange of ions between the bone substance and the external solution rather than upon a unidirectional accumulation or depletion of a single ion species. Fossil bone, therefore, behaves in a manner fundamentally similar to living bone.

Insofar as the determination of the age of fossil bone is concerned, it must be recognized that the inorganic constituents (save perhaps fluorine) are of little immediate value. The composition of any particular specimen as it comes into the laboratory will have been determined, not by the lapse of time since the death of the person or animal, but by the mutual interaction between the bone and the substances in the soil surrounding it, together with the physical conditions characteristic of the environment subsequent to its burial. If a temporal sequence based on changes in inorganic components is to be established, there will be necessary a combined study of the bones and the corresponding soil chemistry.

Fluoride

It was discovered many years ago that fluoride shows great affinity for bone. Subsequently it was shown that the element probably enters the apatite crystal in such a way as to replace the hydroxyl group and thus forms a very stable compound, fluorapatite. As Carnot[32] demonstrated, this accumulation is a function of time, and in many bones derived from earlier geological periods, especially the Paleozoic, the process has nearly reached completion. Even the Pleistocene may show more fluoride in the bone than more recent time shows. As an index to age, however, fluoride is of doubtful

---

[32]Carnot, 1893.

value because the quantity accumulated is dependent not only upon duration of burial but also upon the concentration of fluoride in the adjacent soil solution. Nevertheless, Oakley and others in England have recently utilized the method to establish estimates of antiquity for the Piltdown Man and other well-known fossils.

We have recently performed a few fluoride analyses, using a modification of the standard method of Willard and Winter.[33] This work has only begun, but it is possible to report analyses with reference to bones from three sites: Soda Canyon near Mesa Verde, New Mexico, Sac-6 in the Sacramento Valley of California, and a site of late cultural period in Marin County, California, near the sea coast. Our results all fall within the range established by Carnot for fluoride content of very modern fossil bones. At the same time there is considerable internal variation. The bone from Soda Canyon has an extremely low fluoride level, that from Sac-6 a somewhat higher level, and that from Marin County the highest. These findings are in entire conformity with the corresponding soil conditions, for the Soda Canyon site is in arid country with little opportunity for movement of soil solution, Sac-6 is in a region of relatively low soil fluoride, and the Marin County site is close to the ocean and exposed to spraying and misting by sea water. We have little expectation of establishing any significant temporal sequence, but we feel that the method may have value in differentiating between human and animal bones from the same site and the same horizon. If two such bones were contemporaneous in origin and have been exposed since burial to identical chemical influences, the fluoride content should be similar. Conversely, if the fluoride contents are widely different, this constitutes prima facie evidence of separate origin in time.

Water

The nonmineral fraction of bone has always received relatively little attention on the part of biochemists and physiologists as well as of archaeologists. Yet these may be precisely the materials which will yield the most significant information concerning the process of fossilization and also concerning the time element.

Water is present up to nearly 25 per cent by weight in

---

[33] Willard and Winter, 1933.

living bone and is known to persist in small traces in fossil bone. In our investigation we undertook a year ago to determine its actual quantitative value. After exploration of several methods for determining water content, it was found that the simplest and most reliable was exposure of the bone to a temperature of 90°C. for one day. Almost identical results can also be obtained by desiccation over phosphorus pentoxide. Either method shows that bones which have been kept in the laboratory at room temperature for several months or years contain from 2 to 8 per cent by weight of water. Moreover, the exact quantity is dependent upon the relative humidity of the atmosphere, for the day to day fluctuation found in the same bone sample is very appreciable. Hence it is necessary to equilibrate all experimental material at a constant humidity prior to measuring water content.

If fossil bone is subjected to mild heat or desiccation and the water loss is measured, it may then be restored to the original conditions of temperature and humidity. It thereupon returns within a few days to its previous state. In other words, the water is lost reversibly. This fact demonstrates that at least a large part of the water is held by adsorption on surfaces or by extremely weak chemical bonds. We have called this the removable water. Two further points of interest have emerged.

First, we have correlated the water measurements for some 400 bone samples with the corresponding values for total organic matter (the latter will be discussed subsequently). The coefficient is extremely high, better than plus .90. A similar relationship exists between water and nitrogen. Hence it must be concluded that at least part of the removable water is bound rather lightly to the organic matter of the bone. How large a part is so bound can be determined fairly closely by plotting the actual values for water content against those for organic matter and nitrogen. A straight line is obtained in both cases which intersects the axis for water at approximately the value of 2 per cent. From these results one can assume that 2 per cent by weight of the bone always consists of water which is attached to or incorporated loosely in the mineral fraction, while a variable amount is bound to the organic part, of which, however, it always constitutes a constant proportion.

Second, we have noted that the observed removable water tends to diminish with increasing age of the bone. Thus, if we compare the average water content for 10 late, 6 middle period, and 7 early sites, the respective values are, in per cent of bone weight: 6.03, 4.91, and 3.76. If, however, we deduct 2 per cent as being always attached to the inorganic part, we get the values: 4.03, 2.91, and 1.76. These are statistically very significant differences.

It is likely, therefore, that there exists here a first approximation to relative age. The individual variation from bone to bone is such that no very exact application can be made in the case of a single specimen. On the other hand, we have never observed any extreme variation and consequently a single specimen can be allocated to a general category on the basis of water alone, such as quite recent, moderately old, or very old.

Organic Matter

During life the nonmineral matter in bone, apart from water, consists principally of fat and the protein ostein. Analyses performed in this laboratory some years ago on recent prehistoric specimens indicated that the fat had entirely disappeared. Hence there remains in the buried material primarily the protein, the chemical fate of which becomes of significance to the process of fossilization.

The clearest index to the protein content of fossil bone is the organic nitrogen. This, in turn, is substantially equivalent to the total nitrogen since the latter in the form of either ammonium salts or nitrates is present only in traces. The determination of total organic matter, regardless of chemical constitution, presents certain difficulties. We have in the past utilized a method of approximation whereby the removable water and the carbonate carbon dioxide are subtracted from the loss incurred when the whole bone is ashed. The balance is considered organic matter. It probably includes an unknown amount of water, however, and hence can be employed only in an entirely empirical fashion. We may multiply the nitrogen value by the conventional factor of 6 to obtain the protein, but this procedure is questionable since we cannot be sure that 6 is the correct factor for bone protein or that protein is the only type of organic compound present. We are now working on the determination of organic carbon by various combustion methods. This may yield further evidence which can be employed to compute the true organic matter. In the meantime the data, even when used empirically, have brought to light relationships of interest.

When we correlate the nitrogen values for roughly 400

individual bones against the corresponding values for organic matter obtained by the indirect method just outlined, the coefficient is plus .955. A further modification consists in computing the average value of the organic matter for each class interval of 0.2 per cent nitrogen. When these average values are plotted, the regression between the two components is seen to be almost perfectly linear and $\underline{r}$ becomes equal to plus .995. Moreover, it can be demonstrated that at least 99 per cent of the variance is attributable to the regression of per cent nitrogen on per cent organic matter with only 1 per cent referable to extraneous or uncontrolled factors. Although final proof must await more precise organic analysis, it is nevertheless reasonable to adopt the hypothesis that as the bone protein decomposes during fossilization the nitrogen disappears in a parallel fashion. The constancy of organic composition is also tentatively supported by the few carbon analyses made to date. These seem to show that the proportion of organic carbon in the nonmineral fraction as well as the carbon-nitrogen ratio remains essentially unchanged in all the bone samples.

That there is actually a consistent secular reduction in both nitrogen and total organic matter has been clearly demonstrated. Thus taking again 10 late, 6 middle, and 7 early sites the average organic matter and nitrogen are respectively as follows: organic matter: 17.78, 11.03, 5.99; nitrogen: 2.87, 1.65, 0.73.

The incomplete results to date with organic carbon manifest a similar trend.

During the discussion of the inorganic bone constituents it was pointed out that the fate of calcium, phosphate, and carbonate is contingent primarily upon the chemistry of the soil matrix surrounding the bone and that elapsed time bears no direct relationship. The nonmineral materials, on the contrary, appear to be relatively independent of external circumstances. Some progressive and consistent alteration seems to be in operation whereby the organic substances, particularly protein, undergo slow decomposition with release of nitrogen and water. The nature of these changes is at present completely unknown. Furthermore, the effect on their velocity of the climate and ambient chemical factors likewise remains to be discovered. The fact that local modifications exist must be conceded from divergent results obtained with a few culturally equivalent late sites and also from the close similarity which characterizes certain sites of unquestioned cultural disparity. The principles here set forth must, therefore, be regarded as outlining only the general picture and as having full validity only over a broad statistical range. In the meantime we have found that the nonmineral bone constituents are of considerable assistance in checking cultural estimates and placing many sites in their proper position on the relative time scale. If we could get a few key points from the C^{14} determinations, we could convert the data to a fairly rational absolute scale of time.

DISCUSSION

(Some time was spent on the fluorine technique, but the recent papers by Oakley have since been made available; they are listed in the bibliography. —Editor.)

GRIFFIN: These analyses of yours, would they be applicable in quite a number of areas, including the Valley of Mexico, to test the time relationships?

COOK: I've become a little cautious about applying the method willy-nilly to an area about which I know nothing, after getting out of the Sacramento Valley and finding discrepancies. If the organic matter holds up, it may be possible to extend it geographically.

COLLIER: Do you happen to know anything about the fluorine content of the soil of the Valley of Mexico?

COOK: Not a thing.

BRAINERD: Isn't the fluorine content of the soil waters a determinant in judging age from analysis?

COOK: That is correct.

SPAULDING: In any case, without regard to the soil, you can at least get relative data on whether a series of bones from the same site have the same history.

COOK: Exactly, that's its value.

COLLIER: Providing there is enough fluorine so that you can

make a reliable measure.

COOK: Well, you have to fool around with a few micrograms.

BREW: I think you said, in that last case you mentioned, both horse bones and camel bones: Did the camel bones show about the same results?

COOK: The camel bones showed the same chemical composition as the horse bones.

GRIFFIN: I noticed that you spoke of a graduate student who had done quite a bit of this work and what I immediately wondered was whether there are other physiologists in the country who would be willing to undertake such projects and if their graduate students would be competent to aid in these analyses.

COOK: I don't see why not.

Metallurgical Analyses and Their Aid to Archaeology

William C. Root

There are three principal procedures which can be applied to metal artifacts by chemists and metallographers to give information of interest to archaeologists. These are spectroscopic analysis, quantitative analysis, and metallographic examination.

Spectroscopic examination is the easiest. It requires only a small sample, 0.05 - 0.10 gram, which usually does not injure the specimen for exhibition purposes. From an examination of the spectrogram one can tell of which metals the object is composed and get a rough idea of the amount and nature of the impurities present (silver, tin, lead, arsenic, and so forth).

The results are sometimes surprising. A small disc and a large plaque from the Cenote at Chichén Itzá appear to be made of silver. Actually, they are of tin. Several ornaments and figurines from Panama which appear to be of solid gold are gilded tumbaga. In museums many objects from Peru labeled bronze are copper and vice versa.

The impurities in copper are of particular value in that they frequently give a clue to the origin of the metal from which the object was made. Here are two examples: Wirework bells from the Valley of Mexico and adjacent highlands nearly always contain a considerable quantity of lead. Those from other areas do not. Most of the wirework bells from Yucatan, where there is no metal, contain lead. It is probable that these bells are trade pieces from the Valley of Mexico.

The bells found in the Southwest consist of practically pure copper. There is little doubt that they are trade pieces from Mexico. The only region in Mexico where copper objects are of nearly pure copper is the west coast (Sinaloa and other states). That this is the probable place of immediate origin of the Southwestern bells is confirmed by the fact that they are similar in shape to the bells found in Sinaloa.

This method does not always give useful results, however. Peruvian copper does not seem to have any characteristic impurities, so the many spectroscopic analyses that have been made of objects from Peru have given no information as to their origin.

Quantitative analysis is a more time-consuming operation and it requires from 0.1 - 0.2 gram of material. Its chief value is in determining the composition of alloys of gold, silver, copper, and tin. Here are three examples:

Gold from Colombia has been shown by Lothrop to contain a high percentage of silver (up to 25 per cent), while Central American gold contains only a slight percentage. Many gold objects from Panama are rich in silver. This confirmed Lothrop's previous identification of these particular objects on stylistic grounds as trade pieces of Colombian origin.

Two common artificial alloys are tumbaga and bronze. Numerous analyses of objects made from these alloys indicate that in both cases their composition varies within wide limits. This would indicate that the alloys were made by very crude rule-of-thumb methods and that there was little or no attempt made to weigh out the constituent metals and mix them in definite proportions.

One of the most perplexing problems of ancient American metallurgy is that of soldering. As will be seen later, it was a process that was less used than is commonly supposed. That soldering was sometimes used is shown by the analysis of solder from a gold earplug from Ica on the south coast of Peru. The analysis (in per cent) for the earplug showed gold 57, silver 37, and copper 6; the analysis for the solder showed gold 8, silver 87, and copper 5. It is hard to see, however, why this particular solder was used in this case, as it has a higher melting point than the gold earplug.

Metallographic examination of a polished section of an object is the most difficult of the three processes, but it gives the greatest information about the actual methods used in the production of the object. It seriously damages the object, and it is fairly expensive. But from such an examination one can tell if the metal in the object was cast, hammered, annealed, soldered, welded, plated, or gilded by the process of mise en couleur.

What metallographic analyses can reveal, the archaeologist may best be shown by the consideration of several examples. Most of the following objects were sectioned and interpreted by Dr. Morris Cohen, of the Massachusetts Institute of Technology.

Example 1. Copper rod. Peru.
(Cerro la Mora, lower Santa River. 4.5 mm diameter.
Early Chimu period.)
The photomicrograph showed that the metal exists as severely distorted twin crystals. The presence of twin crystals indicates that the copper has been cold worked and then annealed above the recrystallization temperature of copper (about $200°$ C.). Undoubtedly, the copper was put through this work-anneal cycle several times. The distortion of the twin crystals further indicates that the copper was severely cold worked after the final annealing treatment.

This is the earliest known example of annealing in America.

Example 2. Striped gold collar. Peru.
(A. M. N. H. 41.0-3707. Huarmey. 15 cm wide, 0.55 mm thick. Stripes about 2 cm wide.)
This well-known piece has eight alternating dark and light colored stripes. Quantitative analysis (in per cent) showed for the dark stripes gold 80, silver 14, and copper 6; that for the light stripes showed gold 54, silver 40, and copper 6. The metal was cold worked, annealed, and further cold worked as in Example 1.

Example 3. Ornament of gold beads. Ecuador.
(A. M. N. H. 41.0-471. Esmeraldas. Each bead is 1.4 mm in diameter.)
Analysis (in per cent) showed gold 92, silver 6, copper 2. The ornament consists of eight minute gold beads arranged in the form of a cube, apparently soldered at the points of contact. The photomicrograph shows clearly, however, that they were cast as a unit and were not soldered or welded. The dendritic structure of the gold continues in an undisturbed way through the junctures. They were annealed after casting. This is one of the most remarkable examples of casting that I have seen.

Example 4. Loop from bronze necklace. Mexico.
(A. M. N. H. Loan T 66.5. "Mexico," probably Oaxaca.)
This is now a dull lead color as if of tarnished silver. Actually, it is a bronze of low tin content. A typical unit consists of a "tortoise" with three groups of loops to which is fastened a small ring from which is suspended a long narrow bell.

The photomicrograph shows that like Example 3 the "tortoise," loops and ring were cast in one piece with no sign of welding, brazing, or soldering.

These two cases indicate that much of the apparently soldered or welded filigree work was really cast.

Example 5. Silvered finger ornament. Peru.
(A. M. N. H. 41.1-435. Lambayeque One, grave 1-3. Curved sheet 3.0 by 1.6 cm.)
This object consists of a thin copper sheet with brilliant silver surfaces. The elongated copper structure indicates that it was cold worked. The silver layer is doubled back on itself in several places indicating that the copper was covered with silver leaf. The leaf is only 0.002 mm thick. It was probably fastened to the copper by hammering.

Example 6. Gilded copper bell. Panama.
(Peabody Museum, no number. Coclé. Analysis 427. 2 cm diameter.)
Gold 12 per cent, silver 2 per cent, copper 81 per cent. It has a black fracture. It is gilded on both the outer and inner surfaces. The photomicrograph shows that the metal has undergone almost complete corrosion. This accounts for the black fracture. The gold layer is rather thick (0.02 mm) and etched readily on its inner but not its outer edge. This is what one would expect if an object made of tumbaga was gilded by dissolving the copper from the surface of the alloy (mise en couleur). This also explains the curious fact that the bell was gilded on its inner surface.

None of these methods gives any information about the age of the metal object except indirectly. For example, any Peruvian bronze object comes from a late period. Age must still be found from that of the pottery associated with it or from its style when that is possible.

The chemist and metallographer can thus give the archaeologist considerable information about the metal objects that he finds. When enough of this sort of information has been gathered together on metal objects of known age and provenance, it will be possible for the archaeologist to work out a fairly accurate picture of the development of metallurgy in a given region and eventually in all of ancient America.

DISCUSSION

SPAULDING: Did I understand you to say that the problem of casting versus cold hammering can be decided only by a regular metallographic examination?

ROOT: You can usually tell whether or not an object is cast by looking at it. But you can't tell whether it's been cast and then annealed.

GRIFFIN: Have you looked at any copper objects from the Great Lakes area?

ROOT: I've looked at some of them, but I found those I examined rather uninteresting because they have only silver as an impurity. Apparently, the only process which was used was hammering, so that there isn't much to be found out, really, from examining them.

GRIFFIN: There is not much chance of their being cast?

ROOT: Some of them look as though they were cast, but as far as I know no sections have ever been made of any of them, so you can't tell whether they were or not.

GRIFFIN: There's at least one individual in the United States who thinks that many of them were cast, and I think the sooner that it is determined by unprejudiced investigators....

ROOT: Well, it would be easy enough to tell if they were cast or not.

RITCHIE: Is it necessary to destroy a specimen in order to make that determination?

ROOT: No, not if it were an object that had a neck or projection; a small section could be cut off.

RITCHIE: Approximately how large a piece would you have to have?

ROOT: You ought to have one perhaps a quarter of an inch long, approximately. It doesn't require too much.

SPAULDING: Even if a specimen were cut in two, that would hardly destroy its value as a specimen.

JOHNSON: Have you ever handled any iron?

ROOT: No, I have never done anything with iron.

WARD: I wish you'd preach the gospel to the Near Eastern archaeologists because until recently on most sites they didn't even analyze to find out whether an object was made of copper or bronze. In the Near East we have, I suppose, the first use of metal by man. The textbooks tell us—and one would think it is true—that the first metal artifacts were made of native copper and that they were hammered into shape. As to the next technological stage, we don't know yet whether the native copper was melted for the first casting or whether the first casting came with the discovery of smelting. There is another thing that we should like to know and that is about the earliest production of bronze by alloying. In this earliest bronze was a single ore used, which contained tin as well as copper, or were separate lots of copper ore and tin ore smelted together, or was relatively pure metal of both copper and tin melted together, or was some combination of those processes employed?

ROOT: I don't know of any way of telling from an examination of the object how it was made, unless one found little chunks of ore around some site, which, apparently, aren't often found. Of course, the same is true in Peru where you have bronze; you don't know whether it was smelted or whether it wasn't. There are little objects of tin found there every now and then, but I should think that they were probably native tin, rather than smelted tin.

GETTENS: Did you say anything, Bill, about the purest kind of primitive copper, native copper, that you have found? I raise this question because I have under consideration now the authenticity of a Chinese object. It's copper clad, copper sheathed. One of the things that struck us after we made a spectrographic examination was that there is present no impurity in excess of about one-tenth of 1 per cent, including silver and other things you might usually find associated with copper. Do you find any particularly pure copper?

ROOT: I've found copper which is as pure as that, Southwestern metal, some samples of ore from northern Mexico, and some of this northern material from the Great Lakes region.

GRIFFIN: Would there be any possibility of distinguishing between Lake Superior area copper and the copper you spoke of from northern Mexico?

ROOT: I should doubt it; it doesn't seem that it's very likely. Another thing that makes this very difficult and that makes the analyses less valuable than they seem, is that if you take placer gold, for example, with silver in it, and expose it to running water for a long time, apparently the silver gradually disappears and it becomes purer and purer gold. Thus, if two samples of gold came from the same source and one of them was in the water and the other wasn't, the composition would be quite different by the time the natives picked up the pieces and made the objects. Another thing that fouls it up is that the natives may very well have melted together different pieces; that is, bells from one region are traded into another, and they are melted up with other metals, and then some object is made from the mixture. The result is something which has a composition halfway between the composition of objects found in the two places. It looks as though it were made from a new source of copper, but actually it wasn't.

GRIFFIN: Are these Mexican specimens melted?

ROOT: Most of them have been cast, originally.

GRIFFIN: In the eastern United States, in the Mississippi Valley, we have a succession of typological uses of copper, so that when a relatively pure copper turns up, we say, "Aha, it's Lake Superior copper; therefore, the raw material has been derived from contact to the north." Now, perhaps it will be possible to demonstrate that at some period of the sequence of the use of copper in the Mississippi Valley equally pure copper could have come in from Mexico.

ROOT: I've examined some objects from the west coast of Mexico which seem to be of pure copper, those that Ekholm found down there.

JOHNSON: You have another problem, too, one that's been specifically mentioned only by Byers. In addition to Lake Superior sources of copper, copper is found in the drift in New England. Nuggets found in the Connecticut Valley, for example, vary in weight from a few ounces to two hundred pounds. It confuses the whole question of the distribution of copper artifacts. The fact that they are made of copper does not mean that they had to come from Lake Superior.

RITCHIE: Except that you have to take typology into consideration. Most of the Northeastern copper artifacts with which I am familiar have exact parallels with those from the Wisconsin region, where they are infinitely more abundant.

JOHNSON: Very well, but whether you're trading copper or trading an idea is very important.

RITCHIE: It would seem that at least some of the prototypes must have come by trade in order to be duplicated locally. On the basis of form, distribution, and associations, I suspect they are virtually all importations.

JOHNSON: I think that's outside the interests of the symposium. It's an interesting argument, however.

GRIFFIN: I won't be responsible for explanations in New England, but I shouldn't think that much of the material in the northern Mississippi Valley was derived from float copper because of the tremendous extent of aboriginal digging in the available ore beds in northern Michigan and Isle Royale. To explain the distribution of copper and artifacts by saying that an Indian picked up a casual piece that might happen to catch his eye in the glint of the sun is not too reasonable.

ROUSE: There's also the case of the copper that was obtained by Moore in Florida which he had analyzed. He thought it looked like copper from Cuba. Again, it doesn't make sense in terms of the archaeology, yet it would be worth investigating, if it could be done.

COLLIER: Have you any slags from Peru or Panama?

ROOT: No one has found any slags to examine. No. I'd like to examine some, if any ever turn up.

METALLURGICAL ANALYSES

COLLIER: Have any been recognized from known sites?

ROOT: There are some that were thought might be from parts of Bolivia and Argentina, but I don't know where they are or who has them. That's another thing—you don't seem to find the crucibles and furnaces and this, that, and the other thing, that you ought to find for large smelting operations. A few have been found, but not as many as you'd expect.

BIRD: Crucibles have been found in Chile, but I don't know of any from Peru.

ROOT: I've often wondered what happened to all those things.

BIRD: One other question, do you have anything to say about the comparative purity of some of this very pure native copper and electrically purified copper? Are they of the same order of purity?

ROOT: Yes, I should think they would be.

Applications of X Ray to Archaeology

Paul F. Titterington

Archaeologically, X ray is one of the photographic methods. An X-ray picture or roentgenogram is composed of superimposed shadows, starting in the black, going up through the grays, and reaching a clear translucency. Its diagnostic ability depends upon the differentiation of these shadows, which at times are rather complex.

One of the most important uses of the X ray is to show drillings and other cavities in stone; with the X ray one can find out the type of drilling and just where it is placed. Thus, if one wants to illustrate the drilling with a diagram, he'll know that his diagram is correct. And it is possible to discover such things as the number of starts that were made before a drilling was completed.

I have been able to pick out several fakes by using the X ray. A banner stone was X-rayed, showing that one wing was made of plaster of Paris to give it balance so that it would be even on two sides. With questionable specimens such as these it is possible to X-ray them and thus avoid their mutilation.

In most cases flint is difficult to show, since it is opaque. Sometimes it is possible to paint flint with barium and have it show up on the X ray.

Metal shows up as white on the X ray, but it isn't possible to differentiate, for instance, between iron and copper because metals are opaque to the X ray in direct proportion to their atomic weights. One cannot differentiate the metal, but he can say whether or not metal is shown.

In studying pottery from the X ray it is possible to separate shell tempering from grit tempering. We ran some experiments in which we cut our potsherds in half-inch squares, X-rayed them, made our temper count of the particles visible in the plate, and then broke up the sherds and counted the particles of tempering. We found we had an error as high as a thousand per cent. In analyzing our error we found that, especially in the grit-tempered pottery, we have a lot of quartz which is transparent to the X ray and therefore did not show up on the plates. We can tell the

APPLICATIONS OF X RAY

difference between shell tempering and grit tempering with the X ray, but, of course, that can be done without the X ray.

About all we can expect from X rays of this type is demonstrations of cavities and drillings in pieces, and we have been able to pick out a couple of fakes.

(Dr. Titterington's paper consisted largely of a series of slides illustrating the suitability of X ray for examination of various archaeological materials. —Editor.)

DISCUSSION

WARD: Is there any way to indicate the presence of the flint where the flint is opaque and doesn't show up on the X rays?

TITTERINGTON: I have taken embedded bone and arranged the bone so that the plane of the arrowhead would be perpendicular and the X ray would be going through the longest possible diameter of the blade. You can show faintly some pieces of flint in that way, but what you get is just a straight line of increased density, not any indication that it was an arrowhead at all.

COLLIER: Did you put the specimens in a solution of barium?

TITTERINGTON: I've taken arrowheads out of bones when they were removable and painted them with barium and shown them, yes. I showed a slide of a vertebra in which there was embedded a small arrowhead. Even going through the piece edgewise, I still couldn't show it. The X ray you saw was made through the flat surface.

COLLIER: Do you think that one might put a piece of basketry or sandal construction in a barium solution and get any detail of construction that way?

TITTERINGTON: I X-rayed a basket at the Art Museum in St. Louis, one of the baskets made of coiled grass. I was able to demonstrate its construction very nicely. What one does there is use a very soft ray with a long exposure, as the Viking Fund is prepared to do. With the diagnostic machine that I use for this work, the lowest I can get is thirty thousand volts, while here they can get down to five thousand. I put the object on the floor and put the tube up as high as I could, using a six- or seven-foot distance, which is the same as decreasing the voltage up to a certain point.

Usually there is a place for X rays in museums. I learned that a good many years ago at the Chicago Natural History Museum, where I X-rayed the small tropical fish to determine to what species they belonged by the count of the vertebrae. Before I started X-raying them, they teased these fish apart with needles and made an actual count. It simplified the procedure very much to make the X rays. That was done with a very low voltage and long distance and long exposure period.

WARD: At the Peabody Museum we have a vertebra from a prehistoric Chinese that has an arrowhead in it. Instead of being made of flint, the arrowhead is of copper with an iron shank. Now if that had been X-rayed, would the metal have showed up?

TITTERINGTON: It would have showed up as white as a piece of paper. You wouldn't have been able to differentiate between iron and copper, as I mentioned before, because metals are opaque to the X ray in direct proportion to their atomic weights. That's the reason we use aluminum in the filters in our treatment work, and we use some copper when we get up into high voltages. You wouldn't have been able to differentiate between the metals, but you would have been able to say that there was a metallic arrowhead in the vertebra.

BREW: I think, too, that the nature of your arrowhead makes some difference. I have an X ray of an arrowhead in a vertebrae from southern Utah and it shows up quite clearly.

TITTERINGTON: There must be some metallic element, or at least opaque element, in it. That's the exception and not the rule.

Carbon[14] Dating

Donald Collier

The topic of Carbon[14] dating hardly needs an introduction to this group.[34] Libby and Arnold have discussed the method at a number of anthropological meetings and have published several papers on the subject.[35] There is naturally a keen interest in this method and in the dates for archaeological unknowns already obtained, some of which are widely disseminated among archaeologists. But the time is premature for a discussion of these individual dates.

The history of the C^{14} project falls into three phases. The first phase, which may be called the "Baltimore Sewage" phase, began in 1946. It consisted of checking the hypothesis that natural radiocarbon would be found in living matter. Dr. Libby, Dr. A. V. Grosse, and their associates obtained methane gas from a sewage disposal plant in Baltimore, enriched the sample isotopically, and measured its C^{14} radioactivity. They were able to eliminate other possible sources of radioactivity and concluded that C^{14} was present in living matter.

The second phase of the project was concerned with checking some of the basic assumptions, which I shall discuss presently, underlying the hypothesis that C^{14} could be used to date living things of the past. There were two approaches to this. One was a world-wide assay of living matter to determine whether organic materials from various parts of the world, from various latitudes, altitudes, and geographical situations had the same concentration of C^{14}, and to determine what that concentration was (termed the present-day activity). The second was the dating of some ancient Egyptian and other samples of relatively accurately known age.

The third phase of the project, which is still going on, has consisted of checking the method by dating selected archaeological and geological samples of unknown age. The second and third phases of the project have been very

---

[34]See American Antiquity, July, 1951, for more recent evaluation of Carbon[14] dating.

[35]Libby, Anderson, and Arnold, 1949; Arnold and Libby, 1949.

generously supported by the Viking Fund and by the Institute for Nuclear Studies at the University of Chicago. Early in the second phase the American Anthropological Association and the Geological Society of America formed a joint committee on C^{14} dating. The function of this committee has been to advise Dr. Libby on archaeological and geological problems, to help him select and secure suitable samples, and to promote the work in every way possible.

It should be emphasized that the purpose of the third phase of the project has been a general verification of the method; interest in the dates of particular samples has been only incidental. An effort was made to obtain samples from various parts of the world with authenticated stratigraphic positions and preferably lying in stratigraphic series so that the internal consistency of the results might be checked. In order to carry out this objective several collaborators were invited to take responsibility for formulating subprojects dealing with chronological problems of various areas and to obtain the needed samples. A large number of suitable samples has thus been obtained, and Dr. Libby expects that by the end of phase three, sometime this summer (1950), more than 100 archaeological and geological samples of unknown age from North America, South America, Europe, and the Near East will have been dated.

The facts and hypotheses basic to $Carbon^{14}$ dating and a description of the method have been published by Dr. Libby and his associates. A brief summary is sufficient here. $Carbon^{14}$, which is a radioactive, heavy isotope of carbon with a half-life of approximately 5500 years, is formed in the earth's upper atmosphere as the result of the bombardment of $nitrogen^{14}$ atoms by cosmic rays. The C^{14} atoms thus formed combine with oxygen to form carbon dioxide, become mixed in the earth's atmosphere with the vastly greater proportion of carbon dioxide containing ordinary carbon atoms, and enter into all living things, which, through the life process, are in exchange with the earth's atmosphere. All matter contains C^{14} in a constant proportion as long as it is alive and in exchange with the atmosphere. But when it dies there is no further intake of C^{14}, whereas the contained C^{14} continues to disintegrate at a known rate, so that the amount of C^{14} remaining is proportional to the time elapsed since death. The dating of an ancient organic sample results from the measurement of its contained C^{14} and the calculation of its age from the amount of disintegration that has occurred since death or removal from the exchange relation. This dating is possible on the basis of the present-day C^{14} content of living matter and the known half-life of C^{14}. The laboratory procedure consists of burning the sample, reducing it to pure carbon, and measuring the radioactivity in a specially constructed radiation counter. The age of the sample since death is calculated from the number of counts (explosions) per minute per gram.

There are four basic assumptions underlying C^{14} dating. The first is that cosmic radiation has remained constant during the past 20,000 or more years. If cosmic bombardment was more or less intense in the past than at present, then the rate of production of C^{14} would have been different and living matter at that time would have had a different C^{14} concentration. The second assumption is that the reservoir of exchangeable carbon has remained constant. A significant change in the amount of living matter would affect the proportion of C^{14} in animals and plants. The third assumption is that C^{14} is evenly distributed through the atmosphere and living matter as a result of a long-term process of mixing. And the fourth assumption is that it is possible to obtain ancient samples that are chemically unaltered with respect to their carbon content.

The first two assumptions, concerning the constancy of cosmic radiation and the size of the exchangeable reservoir of carbon, have not been proved absolutely, but there is a high probability that they are correct, at least for 15,000 to 20,000 years. The C^{14} dates on the ancient Egyptian and redwood samples agreed satisfactorily with the known ages ranging from the present to 4800 years ago. This means that these factors were constant for at least 4800 years in the past and very probably for a considerable period before that. The average age of C^{14} atoms in the atmosphere and in living matter is one and a half half-lives, or roughly 8500 years. If, therefore, the present C^{14} equilibrium extends back 4800 years it probably extends back an additional one a half half-lives, or a total of about 13,000 years. The primary aim of phase three of the project has been to test this probability by means of the degree of consistency of the C^{14} dates in regional and world-wide sequences.

The third assumption concerning the mixing of C^{14} and the constant intake by all living matter was confirmed by the world-wide assay. The fourth assumption, that it was possible to obtain unaltered samples, was confirmed by the dates obtained on samples of known age and has been further confirmed during the third phase by cross checks of wood, charcoal, shell, and antler samples of unknown age from the same or related stratigraphic positions.

In assessing the C^{14} method as a whole and the dates on specific samples, it is essential to understand the sources and nature of the experimental error involved in the method. The three principal sources of error are: (1) the determination of the half-life of C^{14} (5568+30 years), (2) the determination of the present-day activity (15.3+0.5 cpm/gm), and (3) the counting error. The counting error in turn is made up of (a) the sampling error, which is the largest error involved, (b) errors in the calibration of the counter and the operation of the electronics (not very important), and (c) the possible contamination of the sample in preparation and handling. Since radiocarbon disintegrations are random in nature, the measurement of a sample involves a calculable sampling error, which varies inversely with the length of the counting run. Dr. Libby's present practice is to measure a sample for 48 hours, this time being divided about equally between measurement of the background radiation alone and the measurement of the sample (plus background). It is this sampling error, given in terms of the standard deviation of the mean, that is expressed by the plus or minus figure appended to C^{14} dates. It is to be read as meaning that there is one chance in three that the error is larger than that shown (one sigma) and one in twenty that it is larger than twice the error shown (two sigmas).

The present method of counting samples directly, called by Libby "rough-dating," is effective for ages of 15,000 to 20,000 years. With older samples the error becomes too large. With enriched counting (isotopic enrichment or concentration of the sample in a thermal diffusion column) it will probably be possible to obtain useful dates back to 30,000 years. Enrichment will require substantially larger samples.

In gathering samples it is absolutely essential not to treat them with any organic preservative. If the sample crumbles it is unimportant. In packing, the sample should not come in contact with excelsior, cotton, or other organic fibrous material that might become mixed with or embedded in it. Rootlets or other intrusive organic matter must be completely removed from buried charcoal and the like if the sample is to be usable. Active decomposition of the sample should be avoided by drying it. It is desirable to seal up the sample in a plastic bag to avoid possible contamination.

It is impossible to state precisely the weights of different types of samples required for dating because the carbon content varies so widely. It is necessary to have 8 grams of pure carbon for one counting run, and it is desirable to make two runs on each sample (total of 16 grams) to check the results. There follows a list of the approximate weights of different types of raw samples required for one run (rough dating), based on present experience.

Plant material and wood	40 grams
Charcoal	12-80 grams
Clean (well preserved) shell	120 grams
Antler (not fossilized)	1 pound
Burned bone	several pounds?
Dung	150-200 grams
Peat	80-300 grams

It is expected that the third phase of the C^{14} project will terminate during the summer (1950) and that all of the dates obtained and an evaluation of the method in terms of archaeological and geological evidence will be published shortly thereafter. In the meantime, several different universities are actively interested in the subject or are in the process of establishing C^{14} dating projects, and it is hoped that within a year at least two of these will be in operation.[36] The approximate cost of rough-dating equipment is $5,000 to $7,000. Operation would require the services of a high-grade technician and the active supervision of a physicist or radiochemist experienced in radiation counting.

---

[36] At the present time the University of Michigan, California Institute of Technology, Columbia University, and Yale University have Carbon[14] counters in operation or in the planning stage.

Ceramic Technology as an Aid to Cultural Interpretation Techniques and Problems

Frederick R. Matson

I'd like to follow the accompanying outline this morning because in that way we can cover a broad field quickly, not spending too much time on any one subject. This is a general view of at least my conception of ceramic technology and the way it fits into the broader view of culture complexes.

Role of ceramics in archaeological studies
    Ceramic culture content - pottery, figurines, glass, glaze, brick, plaster, mortar, cement

Traditional approach in ceramic studies
    Shape
    Decoration
        Shepard's design analysis

Technological approach
    Purposes
        Better understanding of the problems faced by potters in selecting suitable raw materials
            Working the tempered clay
            Drying - taboos
            Slip and pigment decoration
            Firing - selection of fuel, design of kiln, firing procedure, taboos
            Postfiring decoration
            Designing for use
    (A similar outline could be made for glassmakers)
    Objective ceramic description
        To characterize the ware by physicochemical and optical measurements
        To differentiate local and imported pottery
            Itinerant potters
            Imported clay
    Evaluation of the ware
        In terms of the use for which it was intended
        In the historic development of ceramic processes

Techniques
   Study of the properties of the plastic local clay and related raw materials
   Firing of local clays and refiring of clay objects
   Remelting of glasses and glazes and the preparation of synthetic batches
   Physical measurements such as color, strength, hardness, porosity, specific gravity
   Chemical spot tests to identify materials
   Complete chemical analyses in rare cases.
   Optical
      Use and limitations of binocular microscope
      Use of petrographic microscope
         Powders - mineral and glass identification
         Thin section - identification and textural relationships
         Quantitative estimate of tempering material
      Use of spectrograph
   Statistics
      Color analysis - clue to degree of firing
      Binocular sorting with respect to texture
   Ethnological records of manufacturing processes and traditions
Application of techniques
   Formulation of the archaeological problem
   Selection of the most profitable technique for the problem
   Representative nature of the sample
   Effect of burial and soil conditions on the ware
   Time and funds available for the work

Cultural value of ceramic technology
   To help solve immediate archaeological problems
      Identification of materials
      Objective description of ware
      Attempted recognition of imported products
   To help understand the role of the potter in the community and the function of ceramic products in the culture
   To trace in detail the ceramic development at well-stratified sites, relating the data to other phases of the technological development in the culture
   To trace in detail the ceramic technological development in broad regions such as the Near East, China, and Meso-America
   To follow its relationship to the development of metallurgy in order to integrate this sequence into the broader picture of the economic development of a geographic region.

It is not necessary to spend any time discussing with this group the importance of ceramics in cultures, but I should like to indicate some of the items that people at times do not think of as belonging in the ceramic category. Besides pottery and figurines, glass is, of course, fairly important in some parts of the world. Glazes are very closely related to glass in their physical and chemical properties; in fact, the earliest glazes were probably just glasses applied to pottery. Bricks are fairly abundant in some regions. In the Southwest the inclusions found in sun-dried bricks or adobe can be used for dating, and the same thing is true in the Near East. The firing of bricks ties in very closely with the technological development of ceramics in the Near East and in parts of China, and the shape, size, and tempering materials of bricks in buildings of the Roman Empire serve as dating criteria. Mortars and plasters vary a great deal in their chemical and physical properties in different periods and in different parts of the world; the pigments used to decorate their surfaces are also of technological interest. The compositions and properties of the cements that were so widely used in Roman construction are also ceramic problems.

The traditional approach to ceramic studies has been in terms of shape and decoration. An additional technique has appeared in the last few years with Anna Shepard's work on design analysis.[37] This would seem to hold great possibilities for many regions when more people master the technique and when it is applied to nonlinear designs, if that is possible.

Under the general heading of technological approach, I should first like to indicate some of the problems of ceramic technology as applied to pottery. Most important is the need to understand better the problems faced by the potters in making their ware. What were the raw materials available in the region? Did the potters necessarily use clays that were obtainable near the site or did they dig them at some distance? Did they have traditions and techniques that limited the selection of clay despite what was available geologically? When they got the clays, was it necessary to purify them, or had clays been selected that were freed from gravel and other impurities by natural water action? If they did purify them, at what period in cultural development did this levigation of clays first appear, so far as we can tell from examination of sherds? When they added tempering materials what ingredients were selected? This involves not only the identification of tempering materials in the pottery, but also consideration of them in terms of the geography and geology

[37] Shepard, 1948.

of the region. Were the materials selected because of cultural contact with another region in which they were used or because of inherited traditions in the potters' own area? Some ingredients might be incorporated in the clay mass regardless of any technical possibilities inherent in them. Traditional techniques might dictate the use of tempering materials even if good pottery could be made without them.

When the vessels were drying, what problems did the potters face? Did the pottery shrink rather rapidly and therefore crack if the rate of drying was not controlled? A consideration of the shape of the wares, the sandiness of their texture, and the temperature and humidity in the region might give some indication of the drying problems. Of course, from the ethnological accounts available it is known that there are a lot of taboos related to the selection of raw materials and the drying and firing of clays. For instance, pregnant women who passed by while the potter was working, a funeral procession, or many other conditions are always assigned the responsibility for any mishaps, any cracked pots that might occur. I think that a recognition of the restrictions and explanations in terms of taboos, insofar as we can get them, is rather important in considering the potter's relationship to the materials with which he worked. In firing the ware the selection of fuel is fairly important because it will, to a large extent, control the nature of the atmosphere in the furnace. A reducing atmosphere, which was probably quite smoky, would result in a gray or black ware, while an oxidizing atmosphere would cause yellow to reddish brown colors to develop. The design of the furnace and the nature of fuels available would, to a large extent, control the firing atmosphere. The cost of fuel in various regions and at different times in the history of a site would also tie in. After wars there was little desert brush available in arid regions, such as parts of the Near East, because soldiers who had encamped in the area had used up the permanent fuel supplies. It was therefore necessary to float wood for fuel down the rivers, greatly adding to the cost of firing a kiln. Did this difficulty tie in with, perhaps, a lower firing temperature for the pottery after a period of economic unrest? Decoration is a big field in itself, and we can just make a nod in its direction. Decoration before firing and after firing the ware, the techniques involved, and the traditions, as well as the actual identification of the pigments that were used in prefiring and postfiring decorations, the variation in the pigments with time, and their economic significance as related to surface coloration variations in firing traditions all should be considered in a study of ceramic decoration. This brief outline illustrates some of the problems involved in considering a pot from the potter's viewpoint. A similar outline might be prepared for the glassmakers. This would be more complex, because they faced many problems that the potters themselves never had to consider.

A second important purpose in ceramic technology is objective ceramic description. This is the phase in which many archaeologists are interested. It is possible to describe ware objectively by means of chemical tests, optical measurements of color, physical tests, and mineralogical studies, but I often wonder, so what? A nice objective ceramic description appears in the report, but how many people ever take the time to read or try to visualize the pottery once it has been thus described at the cost of much time and expense? Perhaps a little less time spent on the ceramic description in terms of physical measurements, and more consideration of the variations of the ware as related to the manufacturing problems of the potter would be quite profitable. Most archaeologists are interested in identification of imported wares in order to differentiate them from the local ware. Some think of this as a primary problem in ceramic technology; it is certainly a fascinating one, but is often very difficult to solve, for in many areas there were itinerant potters wandering from site to site. Linné has reported them for Peru; they are still traveling around in Greece and in Crete today, sometimes using local clays, but always transporting their techniques from region to region. Clays were brought from China in the eighth century A. D. to Kashan and to other areas of Iran. Thus the importation of special clays which were then mixed with local raw materials complicates the problem of identifying imported and local wares. Subtle differences in shape and decoration, recognized through the study of large well-excavated sherd collections, may be the primary means of establishing ceramic imports. Such selection can then be tested by technical means, but the laboratory study may not give positive result. I am not trying to disparage ceramic technology, but I want to suggest that there are fruitful uses of technological studies other than those traditionally employed which can yield profitable results without great expenditure of time and money.

Finally, after considering the role of potter in his

community and the objective description of the ware, it might be well to try to evaluate the ware itself in terms of the uses for which it was intended in the community and its place in the historic development of ceramic processes. How does the local problem of ceramic development fit into the broader technological scheme of ceramic evolution in various parts of the world?

A great many techniques have been tried in ceramic studies; many more will be used in the future. The study of the local clays and the related raw materials while one is in the field could be extremely fruitful, yet it is a technique that is seldom recognized and has been least applied so far. The inclusion of a person interested in technical ceramic problems in an archaeological field party so that he could spend some time at the site studying the raw materials available would be very helpful. This is in line with the discussion yesterday of the desirability of having some of the technical people in the field to relate the archaeological and the technical aspects of the problem. Unless one is familiar with the local clays of the region I don't think he can do a very thorough job when studying the pottery. It doesn't always help to write back and ask a local workman for a cigar box full of clay. We've tried that and find that there are rather strange concepts as to what constitutes clay and what is a good sample. Perhaps it's even better not to be misled by samples such as that.

The firing of local clays and the refiring of pottery and figurines can often supply very useful clues as to the properties of the pottery and the firing temperatures that were used. There is a great deal of color variation possible in most clays. I thought you might like to see one example, a clay from the banks of the Tigris River. The grayish tan color of the raw clay turns to black upon firing at low temperatures because all clays have a fair amount of carbon in them. It then changes to salmon or reddish brown at around $800°$ C.; when fired a little higher, it becomes yellow; at still higher temperatures one gets yellow-greens and finally greens. This is the range of colors found in the pottery and figurines in central Iraq. Yet when I first tried to duplicate the colors that occur in the sherds, I couldn't do so until I realized one day that I was being too scientific about it, correctly using distilled water, mixing it with the clay as one would in normal technical studies. The Tigris flows over several bitumen beds and sulphur springs and contains a nice concoction of salts, as well as organic matter; the water is consequently so bitter that the Arabs in central Iraq will not drink it if they can possibly avoid it. They go to canals and use water coming from the Euphrates. When I mixed up a brew containing sulphates and chlorides and used it to temper the clay, I had no trouble producing the colors desired. This technique of firing the local clay and refiring the pottery itself under controlled conditions at different temperatures will supply information that can then be used in studying the problems and techniques of the potters. For example, we took about 4000 sherds and partial and complete pots from Seleucia, a site which is on the banks of the Tigris just south of Baghdad, and sorted them in terms of their color. About 70 per cent of the ware was yellow. We broke down the sample into material from different field seasons and from various levels at the site; still the figures came out remarkably constant. I think we had a fair indication of a stable technique over a wide period of time. Yet in one period in that site there was a change. The people of Seleucia, the Hellenistic capital of the Near East, revolted against the Parthian overlords for seven years during which time there was a great deal of unrest. At the end of that period the Parthians tightened their hold on the city with the result that there was a very marked change in the culture. The architecture, the coins, the pottery, and most other material phases of life became Oriental in style, whereas they had formerly been Hellenistic. At the same time there was a marked lowering in the firing temperature of the pottery. One can theorize, and have a wonderful time doing it, as to the reason for this, — shortage of fuel, killing off of the potters, apprentices doing the work, the lowering of standards of value, or economic conditions. You can go on and on. It was established that there was a lowering of the firing temperature of the ware at that time, and although it might be left to others to attempt an accurate explanation for this, I think it's fun to play with the data and see what can come out. Throughout the whole course of the occupation of Seleucia, the figurines were fired at a lower temperature than was the pottery. There is good statistical evidence for this.

    The same approach can be used with glazes and with glasses, but in a much more limited range. Here are some fragments of ancient glass, pieces from Corinth, that were remelted to temperatures at which the glasses would soften.

This experiment gives a rough idea of the minimum temperatures used by the glassmakers. Breaking off a small chip from a fragment of glass in a collection is perhaps not too destructive because one can't use many of the fragments in museum exhibits anyway.

Physical measurements, such as that of color, can be very useful. When an objective description of color is tied in with the firing of clays from the site and the refiring of sherds, its inclusion in a report is then well justified. If the sherds from a site have a range of colors, locating the extremes as well as the average and correlating these data with the properties of the clay will give useful results. But it is questionable if it is worth while to go into great detail in the objective listing of a long series of color numbers in most reports. It makes a nice record, but anyone wishing to compare the ware later with that from other sites will borrow some sherds or go to a museum and look at the pottery and ignore the numbers in the reports, so why take the time to measure them all just to be objective?

Measurements, such as hardness, have been made in great detail, and I'm sure they will continue to be published for a long while, yet when one looks at them in reports and sees what they have contributed to an understanding of the ware, one becomes a little skeptical as to their value. Hardness is a nice, easy, objective physical measurement to include in a study. Yet one can take a given clay from a region and make a pot out of it with a certain degree of hardness in the dry state; then he can compact the surface by using a little water and rubbing it with the hand, a polished pebble, a spoon, or a piece of skin and can thus increase the hardness. Salts in a clay can alter the hardness, but firing temperatures within the range normally used by most primitive peoples have little effect on it; therefore hardness measurements in themselves are not of much use. The same can be said for the porosity of pottery. At one time I thought that porosity would be a very useful tool and made an extensive series of measurements, but it doesn't vary enough from region to region to be really significant. Yet if one finds degrees of difference in the firing of a ware, particularly in more highly fired wares, porosity values could be significant. Like hardness it could be a useful tool when limited to specific applications.

Other physical measurements that can be readily made are tests for strength and specific gravity. There are many variables affecting the strength of a ceramic body, and it is difficult to obtain accurate values because of the curved surfaces of sherds. Changes in specific gravity may indicate approximate firing temperatures, but these can usually be estimated equally well from the surface and cross-section color of the sherds.

Spot tests offer another helpful technique in the nondestructive study of ancient materials. They are particularly applicable to glasses and glazes. A spot on an obscure surface of a vessel can be tested, one that will not mar the piece for exhibition, or a small chip can be removed and used for these chemical tests. It is possible to determine the presence of lead (its use was an important step forward in glass making), whether tin was used to produce opacity in white glazes, and what metallic colorants were used, such as copper, cobalt, iron, and manganese, to produce blues, greens, yellows, purples, and blacks. Much qualitative chemical information can thus be obtained by dissolving the surface area of a small bit of glass or glaze and then testing it with certain reagents. A slightly etched surface results in the small area tested, but this is seldom an objection if it is done on the back of the piece. Of course, it is better to work with fragments, for then much more material representing many vessels can be studied.

Complete chemical analyses have been published for some materials. They are useful in studies of glasses and glazes when the material tested is properly selected, but for pottery they are a complete waste of time. A piece of pottery consists of clay with mineral inclusions; it is not a uniform material. The analysis of one sherd from a pot may differ from that of a sherd from the other side of the same pot, particularly if the clay was tempered and the grain size of the minerals varied. A chemical analysis of a sherd merely states the sum of the constituent elements derived from the clay and other minerals and gives no information as to their relative proportions in the body. In several cases analyses have been published unaccompanied by any interpretation, an expensive and useless nod at objectivity. The time and money spent on the chemical analyses might better have been used on other aspects of the technical study of the materials.

You will note that the use of the microscope has been placed near the end of the list of techniques. This was done because it is the one that has been most widely used so far. It might be well to emphasize other possible approaches, for the availability of microscopists is limited, and other techniques of studying pottery can produce results that will satisfy most archaeological needs. The binocular microscope which has a magnification of from six to twenty can be used by students without special training and is an indispensable instrument in any archaeological laboratory. When one is not available a hand lens can be substituted. The surface finishing techniques used on vessels can best be studied under a low magnification. The only good way to examine the core is to break off a corner or edge from a series of sherds with pliers so that a freshly exposed surface is presented. Then the texture, the range in size, quantity and type of tempering materials, and the degree of firing of the ware can be evaluated.

The color of the core in cross section tells much about the firing of the pottery. At low temperatures the core will be black because the organic materials in the clay have been carbonized; at slightly higher temperatures or with a longer period of firing, the surface layers will be oxidized and will be buff to reddish brown; with further increases in time and temperature (these are dependent linked variables in ceramic firing processes) the entire core may be oxidized to the color earlier developed on the surfaces. In some cases surfaces have been intentionally blackened after the ware has been fired; this technique can be recognized by the occurrence of an oxidized core with black surfacing. It was used at Moundville, Alabama, and was well known in the Middle East, Greece, and Egypt.

You might be interested in seeing this series of small briquettes that have been cut in half to show the color changes that occur as a clay is fired. The raw clay darkens, becoming black at a low temperature, then in successive stages the surface is oxidized, but the black core remains until higher temperatures have been reached and there has been additional firing time. Sherds can also be refired to make possible a study of their color changes. It is easy to make such tests with raw clay and sherds from a site and to correlate the data with the evidence from the cross-section study of a series of sherds under the binocular microscope. The texture of the clay will have some bearing on the color development. Here is a sectioned briquette which has a very black core. It was made from extremely fine-grained clay from the Tigris River, and the carbon is much slower in burning out than it is in more sandy-textured clay, such as that in the briquettes you are examining. A statistical sorting of sherds under a binocular microscope can give much information about the texture, tempering, and degree of firing of the pottery types and sequences being studied.

The petrographic microscope can be a valuable research instrument in archaeology when used by people with sufficient mineralogical training and an interest in archaeological problems. The tempering materials in the pottery and the natural mineral inclusions in the clay can be identified, textures can be characterized, and sometimes local and imported pottery can be differentiated. If one has a good knowledge of the pottery and clays of an area in terms of their mineralogical characteristics, it is occasionally possible to identify the place of manufacture of imported ware. The classical work of Miss Anna Shepard in the study of Southwestern and Central American pottery by microscopic and chemical techniques has been marvelous and needs to be much better known and used.[38] Here is a thin section of pottery prepared for microscopic study. You will note that it is tissue-paper thin, is cemented to a glass slide, and that light can pass through it. In the unique circumstances under which Miss Shepard works the application of thin sections has been most profitable in wonderfully augmenting the knowledge of some phases of the cultures which she has been studying. But one is quite limited in the number of groups that can be studied in this way because of the time consumed, the expense, and the lack of an adequate sherd sampling for thin sections.

The microscope can be used to determine quantitatively the amount of tempering material in pottery by a rather tedious scanning and counting technique. In this way some standards may be established by which similar materials can be classified. With shell-tempered pottery it is easy to estimate the approximate amount of tempering added by dissolving the shell in hydrochloric acid. I have also broken up some soft, sandy, grit-tempered Fort Ancient sherds, actually picking out the coarser tempering materials. Then, with sieve separations of particle sizes it was possible to approximate the amount of grit in the pottery.

When one is through with this work he cannot help wondering, Is it worth it? What difference does it make how much tempering material was in the pottery unless the

---

[38] Shepard, 1936, 1942.

information can be tied in with the working properties of the clay used at the site? Did the clay need tempering because of its stickiness and excessive shrinkage that would cause cracking on drying? If not, why were weathered rock, shell, crushed sherds, ptarmigan feathers, asbestos, or some other of twenty to thirty different ingredients added to the clay? If they were not particularly needed for technical reasons, do they represent cultural traditions and if so, what is their geographical and time distribution? For example, at the Younge site in central Michigan[39] the pottery was tempered with coarsely crushed rock. Some vessels had the inner face plastered with rock fragments as a surfacing. There was no technical function for this rock, as the clay was quite sandy and the addition of rock made it difficult to fashion the vessels. Here was an inherited unquestioning use of a technique that perhaps came from another region or had been used elsewhere with finer-textured clays. It is significant that the clay pipes made at the Younge site were not tempered. The cultural importance of tempering materials needs much more consideration.

Spectrographic analyses are particularly useful in the study of glasses and glazes and in the identification of some minerals. The chemical constituents can be determined from a 0.1 to 0.3 gram sample, and under special conditions it is possible to determine the approximate amount of the several elements present. Such work has to be done by qualified physicists or chemists whose interest in archaeological problems can be aroused.

Statistics are an essential tool in the technological study of pottery. Their application in the study of the degree of firing, the texture, and the tempering material has already been indicated in connection with the use of the binocular microscope. The technique has been used in the study of a large body of Chalcolithic and Bronze Age sherd material from Tell Judaidah in northern Syria. It has also proved helpful in the study of Hellenistic and Parthian pottery from Iraq.

Ethnographic accounts of pottery manufacture can supply some details that may be helpful to archaeologists working in the same region. Such reports are usually disappointingly incomplete because the observer had little interest in or experience with pottery. Even so, useful clues may be gleaned

---

[39] See Matson in Greenman, 1937, pp. 99-124.

that will help explain the characteristic appearance of some sherds from the same region. For example, at one level at Tell Judaidah a ware was made that was full of fine holes which had been formed by the burning out of some organic material. Mr. Volney Jones, an ethnobotanist, studied the materials but was unable to identify the plant remains from the holes that they had left in the clay. Finally, we obtained a clue in a brief account of modern pottery making in remote mountain towns in northern Syria. There cattail fuzz is one of the tempering ingredients used. Such material, when mixed with clay and fired, fairly well duplicates the appearance of the holes in the sherds. Thus, a traditional technique has remained in use for at least 4000 years because of the limitation of raw materials available and the unquestioning use of established techniques. A re-examination of ethnographic literature might aid in the technical study of pottery.

In applying the techniques of ceramic technology to the study of archaeological materials one of the most important considerations is the formulation of the archaeological problem. This can be achieved only by close co-operation between the archaeologist and the technologist. Of this I am sure everyone in this room is convinced; otherwise you wouldn't be here. It takes time to develop a clear understanding of the problem by both parties, but until this is done the selection of techniques of study that will be most profitable cannot be made. It would be silly to apply all of the possible techniques to the study of any one type of pottery except, perhaps, in a training course for graduate students. Ideally, the technologist should spend a season at the site studying the raw materials and working with the large quantities of sherds that can never be hauled back to the museum.

Missionary work is still needed to convince some archaeologists that technical studies have to be co-operative projects. When one gentlemen came back from the field with large quantities of pottery, he brought in a few sherds and said: "I am going to give you one piece of each of my ceramic types, and I'm going to tell you nothing about them. Let's see what you can do with your technical studies."

Having agreed upon the nature of the problem from the archaeological and technical points of view, and having tentatively selected the approach that it is hoped will most rapidly and effectively produce worth-while results, the next major step is to select a representative sample for the study. This is not easy to do because of the restrictions on the materials that can be used for testing and possibly because of the basis of field selection of materials to be shipped home. This point needs no elaboration for it is obvious that one thin section is not going to give much information about pottery manufacture at a site.

Soil conditions can affect the appearance and properties of pottery and glass. If ware containing limestone or shell is buried in an acid soil, these ingredients will disappear. At another part of the same site conditions may be neutral or basic and "hole tempered" sherds will not appear, yet both were originally the same type of pottery. The drainage pattern in the soil plays an important role in leaching the sherds or in depositing salts or calcareous materials on and in the pottery. Refiring studies of such ware can give misleading results.

The time and the funds available for technical studies are usually quite limited. Such work cannot be done quickly, and usually has to be carried out evenings and week ends by technologists who are swamped with their own professional responsibilities. These factors can very strongly affect any decision as to the scope of the problems to be studied.

Technical ceramic studies can be justified only in terms of the contribution they can made to a more complete understanding of ancient cultures. Miss Shepard's work has amply demonstrated their value. Few studies as broad as hers can be undertaken because of the time and costs involved. On a smaller scale work can be done to help solve archaeological ceramic problems through the identification of materials used, the objective description of the ware, and through the attempted recognition of imported products in terms other than those of shape and decoration. This is only a starting point, however, although a very time-consuming process. I think that the basically important contribution that is being made is the help in achieving a better understanding of the role of the potter in the community and the function of the ceramic products in the culture. Foster's work at Tzintzuntzan[40] is an excellent example of a study of a modern pottery-making group in a community. With such a study as a starting point it may be possible to read more into the archaeological data from that region.

[40] Foster, 1948.

DISCUSSION

STRONG: I'd like to call attention to Tschopik's latest paper on Aymara pottery in a recent number of American Antiquity.[41] You may not have seen that. It's like Foster's, but goes back into archaeology.

MATSON: I'm very glad to know that.

In a few cases where it has so far been possible, important results have been obtained by tracing in detail the development of ceramic manufacturing processes at well-stratified sites which have been sufficiently documented with sherds. These results can then be related to other phases of the technological development in the culture, such as metallurgy, sculpture, textiles, or architecture.

Eventually we hope to be able to follow the ceramic technological development in a few important areas, such as the Near East, China, and Middle America. These data can then be used to trace the relationship of ceramic development to that of other crafts, integrating the technological progress into the broader picture of the economic development of the region.

STRONG: Mr. Matson has touched on most aspects of ceramics and yet he hasn't told us why the Plains Indians so consistently broke all their pots. I think that is about the only problem he hasn't touched on. As mentioned before, both Foster's study of Tzintzuntzan ceramics and Harry Tschopik's latest article on Aymara pottery making in the American Antiquity are very illuminating articles. They touch on many of the things of which you have been speaking.

---

[41]Tschopik, 1950.

The Use of Mathematical Formulations in Archaeological Analysis

George W. Brainerd

There has been no recently published critique on the use of mathematical formulations in archaeology. Various qualifications applying to the use of mathematical techniques in general may be profitably reviewed here as an introduction to those of specific applicability to archaeological usage: (1) Statistical formulations are simply a tool for the easier handling of complex and voluminous data; they are incapable of value judgments and answer a problem objectively only in terms of the data submitted. Theoretical concepts must be framed for statistical as well as for all other analytic techniques, and statistical techniques must be formulated and controlled to answer correctly the questions asked. Statistical studies solve the problems of where and when; for the hows and whys we must generally use other techniques.[42] Statistical studies are of great value during the generalizing phase of a study, both for the formulation of the material and for the expression of results, particularly when the data are voluminous and complex. (2) Statistical manipulations have their only connection with reality by way of the systematics from which the manipulated symbols are taken. Archaeological taxonomy is in itself a generalizing procedure which ultimately depends for its validity upon the archaeologist's success in isolating the effects of culturally conditioned behavior from the examination of human products. Each stage of the tenuous sequence from artifacts to culture reconstruction must be controlled and constantly examined to check its validity before final results are acceptable. (3) Mathematical formulations are not universally applicable. Certain types of contextual evidence obtained in archaeology are difficult if not impossible to classify, or if classifiable they are difficult to formulate for statistical handling. Small archaeological samples also pose problems for the solution of which specially evolved statistical techniques are necessary.

The uses of statistical techniques in archaeological studies

---

[42]See Kosolapoff, 1951.

can perhaps best be visualized as the stages of a theoretical outline of analysis are reviewed. By archaeological analysis I mean the procedure whereby the archaeological finds are placed in the framework of time and space, the initial step in the reconstruction of culture history. It is my contention that analysis as here defined should precede and be held entirely distinct from synthesized culture reconstructions which may depend for their documentation upon preceding analyses.[43]

The first step of procedure in artifact analysis is usually the formulation of types, groups of artifacts, each of which shows a combination of similar or identical attributes or traits. These attributes may include choice of material, technique of manufacture, form, and decoration. If point 2 above is acceptable, the systematics used must have cultural validity in that they must mirror the culturally established requirements met by the artisans.[44] In his search for these tenets of an unknown group it behooves the archaeologist as a scientist to work objectively, free of a priori conceptions. The attributes used in sorting artifacts into types should thus be objectively chosen as those which occur most often in combination in single artifacts. Criteria based upon subdivisions of an attribute which occurs in a continuous range through the material are preferably used only when the distribution curve of the attribute in the archaeological samples shows binodality, and the dividing line for sorting should be drawn between the nodes. By use of the above requirements for type attributes, the archaeologist can objectively describe the cultural specifications followed by the artisans. Statistical procedures for the formulation of, and sorting of specimens into, types satisfying these requirements are feasible, and may in some cases be useful.[45] It seems conceivable also that mathematical studies of attribute combinations may demon-

---

[43] Cf. Brainerd, 1951, for an exposition of this viewpoint and of various others embodied in this paper.

[44] These analyses of stylistic tenets should be carefully distinguished from interpretations as to function of artifacts. Functional interpretations should properly be reserved for the later synthesizing stage of the study.

[45] A statistical technique in use by sociologists (Guttman, 1944) holds possibilities for use in this sort of archaeological analysis and may provide an accurate determination of the validity of hierarchic classifications.

strate more finely cut cultural differentiation without the use of the intermediate concept of types, for types are, after all, simplifications to allow qualitative divion of the material into few enough categories to permit inspectional techniques of analysis. Statistical techniques partly eliminate this need by facilitating the manipulation of complex material.

Irrespective of the manner in which the variation in masses of artifacts is classified for study, synchronic and diachronic variations must be recognized and separated before the archaeological time-space framework can be established. Upon the precise and sensitive solution of this problem depends the documentation of causal relations which make possible the reconstruction of culture history and ultimately of whatever generalizations may be drawn therefrom. The fundamental information for such analysis is to be found in the combination of attributes in, and the associations among, artifacts. The amount of this information available varies with the complexity of the individual artifacts and, if the combination of attributes of the specimens is complex, then it may be possible to construct a time framework from artifacts of unknown or imperfectly known provenience. Association may vary in degree and kind from mere propinquity in surface collections to far closer and more significant associations. A group of associated artifacts may be called a collection. The collection gives the best means of judging what artifact types were used at any single time and place, just as the type allows one to judge what attribute combinations were important in a single milieu.[46]

The temporal sequence of groups of artifacts whose variability shows internal structuring into types and collections has been greatly facilitated through the supplementary evidence of stratigraphic placement of deposits. This evidence, external to the study of the collections, has been used for the setting up of relative chronologies supplemented by "cross datings" of trade artifacts between the stratigraphic columns worked out for separate areas. Stratigraphic evidence, when properly pursued, allows, in addition, the separation of variations due to time change from those caused by other factors.

The effects of time through archaeological collections can also be isolated by internal evidence either through combinations of attributes in artifacts or through association of

---

[46]Ford (1936), in a paper, which to my mind has not received as much attention as it merits, has discussed and utilized several of the concepts set forth here.

attributes and types in collections. Such studies for their rationale use the concept that culture change takes place gradually and that artifact attributes and their combinations into types appear, grow in popularity, wane, and disappear in a more or less independent fashion. In analysis of the presence of a single attribute among a group of artifacts, or of its presence or frequency in a series of unstratified collections, there is no certainty that time, rather than other causes, is the factor responsible; variation is universal among artifacts made in a single time span and is caused by variability in the human population and in the materials used for manufacture. But if there is found to be a constant relationship between the presence, absence, or changing frequencies of several apparently unrelated artifact attributes found in combination or association, a more stringent set of specifications is imposed upon the causal mechanism. The cause of such precisely correlated interrelationships must be linear in nature, and the commonest strictly linear factor operative through archaeological materials is time.[47] Moreover, such constancy of interrelationship among several seemingly independent types or attributes has often been demonstrated in plots of type frequencies through stratified deposits whose variation certainly has been caused by time difference. Orderings or seriations of unstratified collections of artifacts showing concurrent changes in frequency of several types have appeared in increasing numbers during the last several years.[48] Most of them have been ordered by inspection of graphed collections, and have usually been supported and their early-late direction established by supplementary stratigraphic or historic evidence. A technique for more exact and objective chronological ordering by statistical techniques has recently been published by Robinson.[49]

Another ordering technique utilizing the same theoretical basis as the studies described above is that of seriation of grave lots. Petrie's sequence numbers for chronological placement of Egyptian archaeological artifacts represents

---

[47] For discussion of this theory and its applications see Brainerd, 1951. For an example of use of two concurrent variables in a graphic chronologic analysis see Beals, Brainerd, and Smith, 1945, pp. 164-68.

[48] For recent examples see Ford and Willey, 1949, and Rinaldo, 1950.

[49] Robinson, 1950.

perhaps the earliest sequencing of grave lots. Kroeber and Strong's[50] studies of the Uhle Peruvian pottery collections and Lothrop's[51] Coclé sequence provide later examples. The ordering is first determined by the association of certain attributes or, if possible, types in single grave lots, and the absence of association of others. This allows ordering of types or criteria in succession on a basis of presence-absence criteria, and places the associated grave contents in the ordering thus formed. The method is theoretically sound provided that enough concurrent attributes, or elaborate enough types, and, in addition, enough grave lots are used to make certain the linearity of the causal factor. Petrie's sequence unfortunately is marred by the interlarding of certain evolutionistic conceptions used to establish both order and direction of sequence.[52] It is undoubtedly true that the procedure of chronological ordering from internal evidence has suffered gravely in repute from supplementary use of assumed evolutionistic sequences based upon single attributes. Evolutionistic assumptions still seem to be in use for sequencing by classical archaeologists.

The attitude commonly held that sequences based on internal or "stylistic" evidence are of an inferior order to those based on stratigraphy[53] seems questionable on theoretical grounds, providing the internal evidence is extensive and has been properly analyzed. The advantages of ordering collections by objective methods utilizing concurrent variation among attributes and types are many, even though external evidence for chronology in the form of stratigraphy is available. The time scale is bound to be refined by such orderings and carries its own internal proofs of validity. Clues to the tempo of culture change and the determination of occupational disjunctions usually are disclosed, the mass of documented material is greatly augmented, and nonchronological variation is thrown into relief and made available for analysis.[54]

---

[50] Kroeber and Strong, 1924a, b.

[51] Lothrop, 1942.

[52] See the analysis of Petrie's procedure in Massoulard, 1949, pp. 61-69.

[53] See, for example, Kroeber in Bennett, 1948, pp. 117-18.

[54] For a recent elegant demonstration of nonchronological variation in an ordering see Rinaldo, 1950, p. 102, Fig. 21. See Rinaldo, as well as Brainerd, 1950, for amplification of the above-listed advantages of ordering.

Analysis of the kind described above represents a considerable refinement over the now classic system of description by period whereby a series of horizons is described from selected collections, and the bulk of the excavated material, if conscientiously classified, is apt to prove to be "transitional." Some of the superficially apparent accuracy of placement in orderings is nevertheless illusory because of the prevalence of collections representing mixed or relatively long-term deposition. Whereas insufficient sampling of short-term deposits has fathered untenable hypotheses of sudden culture change, as in the Southwest, sampling of chronologically mixed deposits can lead to incorrect assumption of strong regional variation, to shortness of time scale, and to various other misconceptions, which, in many cases, may still lie unsuspected in the literature.[55]

The commonly used procedure for the treatment of mixed and long-term collections in the analysis would seem to be, although I am hampered in this statement by lack of explicit general descriptions of this facet of analytic method, the choice of collections possessing minimum variability of types as chronological anchors, and the discounting of collections showing a large number of types per size of collection. This technique, if it is concise enough to be called a technique, is most necessary in areas where sites were occupied over a long time and is often unnecessary to use when mixing from recognizably widely separated chronological horizons makes its detection simple. A start toward a statistical determination of the relative time span of deposition of single collections has been made as a by-product of Robinson's method of ordering from matrix analysis. A further by-product of the study of such mixing of deposits on long-occupied sites may be the determination of early-late direction in chronological orderings by means of the phenomenon of "progressive mixing," the tendency of recent deposits to contain an admixture of earlier artifacts.[56]

Although much refinement in chronological analysis is possible and will certainly be developed, various acceptable techniques are known and generally recognized for this purpose. The chronological framework is linear, the lenticular

---

[55]Several excellent examples of such errors in analysis are reported to occur in papers on the post-Teotihuacan archaeology of the Valley of Mexico.

[56]See Brainerd, 1951.

curves of growth and decline of type frequencies in a single site through time are predictable and are apparent in ordered collections. The analysis of recognized regional variation, set in a two-dimensional geographic framework and depending upon widely ranging rates and kinds of cultural diffusion, presents a more complex problem; methods for its solution are neither standardized nor well agreed upon.

The analysis of regional culture variation has proceeded, using various techniques in various areas. In the Mississippi drainage the Midwest Taxonomic System has set the methodologically interesting, although questionable, course of analyzing total variability in material culture without an initial separation of that part of the variability due to chronological change. Doubts have recently been raised as to the validity of analyses made under this system, as attempts have been made to fit the gradually emerging chronology of the Mississippi Valley to the framework previously evolved under the system. In the Southwest, the Gila Pueblo and the Museum of Northern Arizona taxonomic systems have attempted to infer regional cultural developments through time by the use of a chronologically documented branching organization of pottery types. The inadequacies shared by these and the Midwest system in their failure to allow for cultural interaction through anastomoses among the branches of the family tree have been discussed at length in the literature.

An additional criticism of these schemes may fairly be made. The schemes given above all attempt definition of degrees of relationship among cultures along rather mechanistic lines based on the relative degrees of similarity and dissimilarity in material culture. If it be assumed that the relationships shown are significant, there still remain questions concerning the nature of these relationships and concerning the cultural interactions which produced the statistically documented relationships. The weakness of this link may have grown initially from the typology upon which these analytic schemes are based. Typology as used in the Midwest and Southwest, and in many other areas, although adequate for present-day chronological sequencing and the tracking of trade which allows the cross-tying of chronologies, still falls far short of full utilization of archaeological materials for the recovery of information on culture. Recognizing this weakness, Rouse[57] has proposed his "modes," selected attributes which

[57]Rouse, 1939, pp. 24-35.

cross typological lines, and which are complex enough to suggest culture diffusion as their cause. Brew,[58] probably with the same technique in mind, has suggested multiple classifications based upon the varying ends in view. Studies in materials, such as pottery paint and temper, design styles, craft traditions, artifact forms, all are susceptible to the use of this technique, and all provide information as to the kinds of regional interrelations with greater facility and accuracy than do classifications built upon artifact types.

The usefulness of the type as a working tool may justly be questioned for purposes other than the determination of a time-sequence scale and of direct trade, for its combined attributes of material, technique, form, and decorative style may well be largely meaningless in the study of culture variation over space, although because of craft tradition and constant source of materials they tend to cohere through time in a single region. The restrictions to complete utilization of material caused by our present sort of typology are under our present techniques justified to some degree by the necessity for such a simplification to keep analysis within the bounds of mental grasp. Mathematical techniques can enlarge these bounds and may provide tools for the more intelligent manipulation of the objective attributes already used in the formulation of our typologies.

The theory which should control the formulation of problems and aid in the interpretation lies in the now rapidly growing ethnological and archaeological literature on the relations of tradition to culture change of various sorts.[59] An increasing recognition of traditional craft techniques from more evanescent, but more widespread, stylistic attributes should aid in the forging of less cumbersome tools for regional analysis than are the present archaeological types. In such analyses, it is conceivable that a bridge may be found uniting the objectivity of the taxonomist to the cultural sensitivity of the humanist. Cultural intangibles can, if they exist, be made tangible. Better technique is the solution.

An archaeological field which has thus far been badly neglected lies in the study of poorly documented and unassociated artifacts. Such materials, selected as they usually have been for complexity of design and fineness of workmanship

---

[58] Brew, 1946, p. 46.

[59] For examples applicable to archaeology see Willey, 1945, and Tschopik, 1950.

are ideal material for the documenting and tracing of cultural influences. The combination of attributes in single pieces acts as anchor points to document such parts of the time-space framework as are not available by comparison with excavated materials, and in addition adds much richness to the archaeological record, both as documentation and in establishing presence of attributes at given times and places. Statistical analysis forms a good tool for the investigation of this sort of material. [60]

As in so many archaeological problems, the solution of this one depends on interrelations with another discipline. Although the mathematical tools necessary at this stage of archaeological analysis are not complex in use, their choice and method of use depend upon a good theoretical knowledge of certain branches of mathematics, in combination with a knowledge of archaeological techniques and their implications. Until such cultural cross breeding can be intelligently directed in our universities, long talks and co-operative projects with mathematicians can provide the key to many problems of archaeological analysis.

DISCUSSION:

RITCHIE: Are you using a correlation based on a single trait, say pottery?

BRAINERD: I'm using a measure of agreement which is derived from some fifteen or twenty pottery characteristics. We only got pottery in these collections; we didn't often get other artifacts. These characteristics are various traits in ware and form of the pottery. This, of course, allows us to separate "mixed" from "pure" deposits in an objective manner and to determine from what horizons the mixed material derives.

If we have a collection which was deposited over a long time span, its profile will usually be low and flat, or degraded, as we call it. In other words, a long-time collection or one which is mixed will show less agreement with its adjacent collections, but will show closer agreement with the

---

[60] Miss Anna O. Shepard is attempting a study of such unassociated data using peripheral punch card records, which provide an exceedingly rapid technique for the assembling of attribute distributions. Such peripheral punch card recording is also in use by the Archaeological Survey Association of Southern California for site recordings.

collections farther from it in the sequence than will a short-span collection. So by means of relative degradation of profile we are able to make some estimate of the relative time span of deposition of each of the deposits.

Another important deduction can be drawn from these matrices. We find that in Maya sites the profiles of agreement of collections placed toward the late end of the sequence tend to be degraded in type, whereas the profiles of the collection toward the beginning of the sequence tend to be of the short-span type. In other words, there is demonstrated in these sites a tendency that I think many of us have noted and used and which might be called progressive mixing. Earth is very rare on Yucatan sites, and people have used it over and over, so that while late collections are all mixed up with earlier material, the early collections tend to be pure. This has given us a way of getting direction of time through our sequences. In Spier's early work in which he made seriations, you remember that he was able to tie his Zuni sequence into history at one end and thus to get direction early to late.[61] But progressive mixing, when present, can also give us quite consistently the direction early-late through our seriations. We've tried a group of graphic models which may give some help on this. We definitely believe that we have been able to separate chronological variations from the various other types of variations within our collections. This technique makes available, of course, for archaeological description, all of the material in collections which we have from these sites. This gives more information than the often used procedure of writing two or three horizon descriptions from the best collections, which are called unmixed, then neglecting most of the other collections as mixed or transitional. This gives you, then, a complete, delicately graded chronology based upon all of your material.

I want to say something more about the punch card, which I mentioned in my talk. All notations such as type of site (there are twenty categories for the type of site), the water source, the location of the site, access to site, condition of the site, whether it's wind eroded, water eroded, all of these factors, a short, critical artifact list, and many other items, are all arranged so that you can indicate the presence or absence of any of them by punching around the edge of the

[61]Spier, 1917.

card. We're trying to list all of the southern California sites on cards of this sort. We have written a small manual to try to get the listing into a degree of uniformity, and then once we have these things punched on the cards, we will be able to pull out of our catalogue of two or three thousand sites all the sites that, let's say, have bedrock mortars in them, or all the sites which have no near-by water source, or any combination of traits, and thus we may be able to straighten out some of this rather amorphous southern California archaeology. Distributional studies can be made very rapidly on any item that is included in the punch card.

Miss Shepard has worked out independently a similar system for listing a whole group of traits which are found on any single piece of Middle American pottery. I believe her concept is to have a card for each museum specimen which is described, and in this way the attributes, which would be roughly analogous to Rouse's modes, could be traced through various masses of materials and their combinations studied, and this would allow, perhaps, the formulation of new typologies, as well as distribution studies on the ceramic material with which she is working.

JOHNSON: Where did you publish this?

BRAINERD: In American Antiquity.

STRONG: It seems to me, Mr. Brainerd, that you covered a very large subject. There's only one thing I would like to ask. Can you tie these bilateral cards in with the Rorschach test?

BRAINERD: No, we haven't got to that. I think we're pulling Robinson in our direction away from the Rorschach.

The Use of IBM Machines in Analyzing Anthropological Data

Frederick P. Thieme

Very frequently the data from scientific research are so considerable that the mere manipulation and arranging of facts present a large, if not the major, problem for the investigator. Certainly the difficulty of handling large volumes of facts is often responsible for delay in achieving results from research. Because of this difficulty some lines of investigation may be neglected, unless there is a reasonable expectation that the results will be fruitful.

The use of mechanical equipment, mostly automatic in operation, is very helpful in solving this common dilemma. This equipment should allow rapid, automatic, accurate, and highly adaptable operations which are adjustable to the particular problems of the investigator.

It is the purpose of this paper to give in outline form the possibilities of International Business Machines and punched cards in analyzing anthropological problems. From this broad general view it is hoped that each archaeologist will see the opportunities for his own individual specialty or problems.

The great effectiveness of the electric punch card method is that once the initial data have been recorded as holes in the cards, the machines will automatically read these holes and perform a wide variety of operations, such as rearrange the cards in any required sequence, transfer data from one card to another, print the information on the cards or on a sheet of paper, consult tables of tabular data, and perform the arithmetical operations of addition, subtraction, multiplication, and division. Electrical impulses through the holes in the cards are used not only to read the data on the cards but to control the operations of the machines. Pluggable connections permit the operator to direct these impulses almost at will.

The standard tabulating card is approximately 3 by 7 inches and stacks 150 cards to the inch. It has 80 vertical columns with 12 punch positions in each column. Of these, 10 are indicators of digits 0 to 9 with the 11th and 12th positions used for codes or for alphabetical punching. As far as recording alone is concerned, it is possible to record as many as 4096 combinations in one column, although this would inordinately complicate the sorting of the cards in practical use. These cards come in standard forms or may be printed specially so that they serve not only as work tools but as permanent data records.

While special calculating equipment has been built for some purposes, the great bulk of the work now being done throughout the country is performed on standard commercial machines. These, of course, have the advantage of ready availability, systematic service, and experienced operators. The following machines are in this category and are listed in their basic operation individually, whereas in many operations they may be combined to perform multiple functions.

The Key Punch is used to record the initial data on the cards. The punching is done manually in one column of the card after another. An efficient operator can punch up to 600 complete cards per day. The cards may be punched alphabetically or numerically and multiple punched in any one column if desired.

The Verifier may be used to check the accuracy of the cards from the key punch, although other methods are frequently used to proofread the cards. In any event, proofreading for recording accuracy is a necessity.

The Sorter is used to rearrange the cards in any desired order according to the data punched on the cards. The sorted categories fall into appropriate hoppers and a counter electrically records the numbers in each group as well as the total card counts. This machine sorts the cards at rates from 400 to 650 per minute, depending upon the model and upon whether or not the counter is used. Of course, numbers of cards in desired categories may be counted for each of any previously sorted groups, thus facilitating the construction of relationship or correlation tables. This machine in many simple operations is the most useful and many anthropological operations need not use any more complex equipment.

The Collator is a more elaborate sorting device. It sorts cards from two hoppers into four pockets according to data punched in several columns. The machine is very flexible and permits the handling of cards according to a complicated pattern giving the comparison of two sets of data for high-low-equal. For example, two packs of cards, each in numerical order, can be merged into a single pack, in numerical order, with one run through the machine. It will test a pack of cards to determine whether they are in numerical sequence according to the data in a selected group of columns (as many as 32 columns at a time).

The Accounting Machine is a large-scale printing and adding machine which reads data from cards, adds and subtracts them in predetermined sets or combinations of groups, and prints the results on a sheet of paper from the accumulated totals in the counters. The machine will add or subtract 80 digits at a time and print as many as 88 digits. It will also print the alphabetically punched cards if desired. The 80-digit capacity may be split up into 16 separate counters and in this way 16 separate groups of data may be totaled and printed at one time if so desired, or 8 counters can be utilized to tabulate the number of individuals in each category group, while the 8 remaining counters can add the cumulative totals in each category for all of the groups. This machine will read cards at the rate of 160 cards per minute and will print 88 digits or 43 alphabetical symbols and 45 digits from each card at the rate of 80 cards or lines per minute. If cards are properly arranged with alphabetical lead cards properly placed, legible tables can be typed directly by the machines and need not be rehandled. These may type in duplicate and automatically space and arrange the lines if desired. This machine may also be plugged into the Reproducing Punch so that totaled results may be automatically punched into cards for subsequent operations where totals may be used instead of the original detail cards.

The Reproducing Punch reads selected data from the cards (or all the 80 columns) and punches them on other cards. It also can be wired to select only certain digits from each column with the result that selected data can be reproduced from multiple punched columns. This device is useful in preparing duplicate sets of cards, in rearranging data on the cards, and in copying data from "table" cards onto the work cards. It has a comparing unit which automatically stops the machine should the reproduced card not be a correct duplicate of the original, and it indicates the column of the error. It can also be wired to punch any desired digit into all of the cards in a desired location. This is all done at approximately 120 cards per minute.

The Interpreter reads the data punched in the columns and prints the information in type on the same card in any desired location across the top of the card or on its face. This makes the data easily read and the card is set into file cards.

The Calculating Punch reads numbers from one or more cards, multiplies, divides, adds, and subtracts them, and records the results on the card or on another card. It has provisions for performing elaborate sequences of operations. It can be adapted to finding solutions to all of the standard statistical formulae, such as means, standard deviations, and standard errors, and these result cards can then be printed in tables or on record sheets. The speed of this machine depends upon the complication of the problem under solution. The Multiplying Punch is similar except that it does not divide, but performs all of the other operations.

In addition, several models of electronic calculators are available in certain establishments. These machines have very high rates of speed and perform complicated sequences and operations. One model of these machines, the 604, can perform 300, 4-digit divisions per minute and consequently can calculate and punch 300 indices per minute from 4-digit data detail entries. Other machines perform square roots rapidly.

All of the machines automatically feed the cards from hoppers into and through the machines into storage hoppers.

The basic operations listed here give the outline of the possibilities of these machines for handling large volumes of data. They can take the drudgery and inaccuracies out of hand calculations and perform rapid sorting of data into useful groups. Their greatest value, however, may very well be that they make it easy to test all possible combinations. Once the data are punched and the operation is being performed, the investigator has only a slight additional labor in trying experimental or exploratory combinations.

It is very desirable that the anthropologist spend the time required to thoroughly familiarize himself with the operation of these machines and that he actually perform the operations himself if desired accuracy is to be obtained. Trained operators are frequently available, but they are not familiar with the problems or the limitations of the data and consequently can never be used in planning the operations and seldom trusted in their actual operation. If the anthropologist cannot operate the machines himself, a system of cross-check operations or repeating should be done to ensure accuracy.

Any archaeological data that can be coded into categories

for which numerical symbols can be assigned can be punched and handled on these machines. Although the machines are designed to handle business and accounting operations, the realization of their possibilities can make them very useful for anthropological problems.

Final Session

A presentation of various cameras and photographic accessories suitable for archaeological and microfilm work was given by Lolita Binns. There was considerable interest and discussion, particularly in the demonstration of the Land Polaroid camera. —Editor.

RITCHIE: It seems probable to me that many people here might be more or less of the same state of mind as myself, namely, impressed with the realization of general incompetence in the fields of so many specialties, while acutely aware of the immense potentialities which all of these specialties offer to the archaeologist. The possibility occurred to me of establishing in the departments of anthropology at some of the larger universities some kind of a short course of instruction for graduate students and for people who have received their degrees and gone out into the field, to teach the basic manipulations of their material in terms of these advanced, and in many cases new, techniques. These courses might be taught by some of the specialists themselves in a manner analogous to that in which surgeons impart special techniques. I thought it might be practicable to set up such courses lasting, let us say, a month or two, to study concurrently or sequentially two or more of these different approaches at each session. I'm sure one couldn't master all of them in one semester.

As an alternative, a board of specialists might be formed to which problems, such as the identification of metals or organic material, could be referred, possibly on the basis of a standard fee. The first plan has the greater appeal to my mind. It might be well to incorporate some of these new special trainings in undergraduate courses for the benefit of students who are now in school, so that they wouldn't have to go back to school and learn them as we would have to do.

GRIFFIN: Would anyone like to comment on either of Ritchie's suggestions?

COLLIER: I'd like to comment on Dr. Ritchie's second suggestion. I'm inclined to agree with him that it's the less fruitful of the two, perhaps for this reason: As a number of people who have talked at this conference have pointed out, the data, that is, the materials that need more special analysis outside of our own field, cannot be separated from their context. It has also been suggested that the most fruitful way of using the technical advances in other fields is through some form of collaboration. I don't see how, if you sent in your corncobs or your pollen or your potsherds to a centralized technical bureau and said: "Please process this for me, I want to know about thus and so," you could get the most out of it. The collaboration wouldn't be close enough.

GRIFFIN: We have had some experience with something like that in our ethnobotanical laboratory at the University of Michigan where Volney Jones receives botanical material for identification and for explanation of its probable uses by the people at the site or in the area. I think that, by and large, it has worked rather well. We also had a somewhat similar idea with regard to the Ceramic Repository. During those fortunate days when we were able to have Matson with us, we had a technological laboratory to go along with the Ceramic Repository. Then there was the lithic laboratory, the late lamented lithic laboratory, at the Ohio State Museum, which embarked on the scheme of identifying materials, particularly flints, as to their source.

JOHNSON: I'd like to stick to the point of having courses in universities. I don't think that it is possible to turn archaeologists into specialists in any one of these different scientific fields. On the other hand, I think that any proper field course, any proper course in archaeology, should outline and demonstrate to students the value, and naturally the necessity, of collaboration with scientists in fields which develop.

GRIFFIN: I think that's quite true. Under the present system in our institutions of learning students of archaeology get their degrees in what is called anthropology, even though there has been some question as to whether American archaeology belongs in such a general heading. That is the way it is now set up. Unfortunately, in most institutions, if an individual gets two courses in archaeology during his eight years, shall we say, of training in college, he's doing pretty well. That is gradually changing now, for at least regional courses are set up, and students are also given courses in archaeological techniques. It is in this type of course, where a broad survey is made of possible uses of techniques in archaeology, that this information could then be given to the students.

There is another way in which that can be done: Those individuals who are seriously considering archaeology as a career can be directed into various fields outside of anthropology for minor fields of specialization, which would receive equal rating at the Ph.D. level with such anthropological specialties as linguistics, cultural anthropology, or physical anthropology. If we could get students at the Ph.D. level to minor in geology, mineralogy, or chemistry instead of linguistics, wouldn't they be just as good students of a particular field within anthropology as if they were forced to narrow down to the five fields which are recognized within anthropology? Within the field of human knowledge, anthropology, I fear, is relatively narrow.

BREW: In this connection, Jimmy, it might be interesting to point out that Mr. Gettens gives a course in the Fogg Museum on "Materials of Art and Archaeology."

GETTENS: We started the course a couple of years ago at the Fogg Museum, but I hate to tell you that it's not being given this spring because of lack of interest in general among fine arts students. Of course, it's the same old story that a lot of people were complaining about here: our fields of knowledge are more or less strictly compartmentalized. In fine arts that's just as true as in other fields, and students hesitate, those who are taking degrees, to go very far up a bypath. Consequently, at the present time, the action does not lie in giving more and more graduate instruction in these allied fields. I'm beginning to feel that the answer lies in specialized short-term courses at a much more mature level, given to persons already in the field.

STRONG: I do not wish to give the impression of being negativistic or too rigid in my interpretation of the present advantages of the fourfold nature of anthropological teaching. I do believe, however, that archaeology, as a cultural study, will flourish best within such a general anthropological framework so far as present conditions are concerned. This being the case, no student can hope to learn the outlines of world ethnology, physical anthropology, basic primitive linguistics, and major in prehistoric archaeology and, at the same time, master higher mathematics, physics, biochemistry, and so forth. It now averages some six years between the A. B. and the Ph. D. in American anthropology. If we add all these other desirable basic science courses with a bearing on anthropology, our Ph. D.'s will be candiates for the old peoples' homes - not for field work or jobs!

Just as the anthropologist who is interested in comparative ethnology will go to sociology and psychology in his acquisition of knowledge, so will the anthropologist who is interested in archaeology acquire knowledge in geology, physics, and other sciences. Our task, it seems to me, is to make the acquisition of such basic but ever-growing, additional knowledge easier in undergraduate, graduate, and postgraduate years. Thus, those participating in a conference like this one, representing technical methodology of a wide variety, might as a result of their considerations organize an allied-archaeological technological board which could be of self-perpetuating but changing nature. If such a technological board did no more than exist on paper, it would have value if a reasonable amount of publicity were given it in the scientific journals, so that archaeologists would come to it for advice. Further, such a board might periodically constitute itself as an institute and arrange to have a technological symposium or series of courses at any of our universities with large archaeological commitments, such as Harvard, Chicago, Michigan, California, and Columbia. A symposium of this sort might be fitted into a summer school curriculum. The work could be divided among such departments as anthropology, geology, and physics, and thus the technical facilities of all could be used, which would probably be lacking in most anthropology departments. This may be a pipe dream, but I believe it would be a perfectly possible outcome if a dynamic technological board, as herein suggested, were to be formed under the auspices of the Viking Fund, the National Research Council, or, perhaps, the Society for American Archaeology.

BREW: There is already a precedent for this. In June, 1949, the National Park Service ran a two-week school in Washington on the preservation of cultural values. This was open to everybody, although it was intended primarily for their own personnel who had to deal with historic houses and archaeological and other types of museums. I attended two or three of the sessions and it was a very good thing. Of course, it

was of relatively short duration, but something like that
could be done; it might be done with different slants in different years.

But to get back to the question of the curriculum. If
we had a situation in which a lot of good jobs in archaeology
were available, there would be more point in recommending
that for some people some of this general coverage in anthropology would not be advantageous. But there are two
factors here; the one that Strong mentioned—it's the only
subject in the whole academic curriculum which views matters as a whole. That's a truism, but it's so. The other
point is that we have to train these fellows to get jobs, but
still most of the jobs that come in are not for archaeologists.
Of course, at the present time with the Missouri Valley
bursting into flame, so to speak, a special situation exists,
but that certainly isn't permanent. That's the crux of the
whole matter as far as the academic setup goes.

GRIFFIN: As I said, we do get degrees in anthropology, no
matter what the specialty may be. For example, the man
who is in physical anthropology should know a lot more about
anatomy and physiology than he does about linguistics. We
recognize that. I don't think, however, that in archaeology
students have been given a chance to absorb as much as they
might in geology, for example, and soil studies. I wish it
were possible to give degrees in archaeology, so that after
his M.A. a student could do special work in allied disciplines
which would heighten his effectiveness as an archaeologist. By
the time he has received his M.A. he should have had sufficiently broad training in general anthropology to be able to
interpret his material from a cultural standpoint.

BREW: We have two students this year, new students in
anthropology, who have had no formal courses in anthropology
at all. But with the spread of anthropology every year, there
are more institutions that give courses in anthropology. We're
still faced with the problem of having entering graduate students who come from places where they've had no anthropological training at all. So your program is still a long way
off, Jimmy.

GRIFFIN: I have one practical suggestion I would like to advance, and that is, in the case of the field of ceramic technology there could be a number of simple aids which could be worked out for archaeologists and distributed to institutions. I have in mind that series of fired clays which Matson prepared. A series of cross sections, or little pellets broken open to show the proportion of tempering material to the clay, comparable to those which he worked up while he was at Michigan could be prepared, and a number of sets of these could be passed around to the various institutions. It would help the archaeologist considerably in his interpretation or judgment of the ceramic material which he gets, and could be accompanied by a statement of explanation. There is something which is on the relatively simple level. If that could be implemented, I think it would be a good idea. What do you think, Fred?

MATSON: I think that would be a good working guide, but it's a little dangerous to put out a color series of clay because the colors of the clay will vary at different sites, and even for, say the eastern United States, the iron content would vary enough so that it wouldn't be a very safe guide.

RITCHIE: True, but you could use it simply as an illustration of what happens with one set of clays at one place. In your manual you could explain your techniques, so that the individual could go locally to his clay beds, make his own potsherds, fire them, or refire them, as the case may be, and compare his results in terms of the standard. You're using it simply as an illustration of the techniques, are you not?

MATSON: Yes, that would be fine to use it as an illustration. That's simply one part of a whole group of things that could be done.

POLLOCK: I'd like to mention that Anna Shepard is working on a general book on ceramics for archaeologists. I think it will cover a lot of these problems. It should be ready next year.[62]

STRONG: I wonder whether either a series of examples of that sort or perhaps an archaeological technical field guide, somewhat after the nature of some of the travel and expedition guides that are available, might fit some of these needs

[62]Shepard, n.d.

of the field archaeologist. It could include a certain amount of tabular and comparative material, perhaps a simple color guide, something on surveying techniques which are particularly applicable to archaeology, and the whole mass could be bound into the form of a short field manual.

COOK: There is only one field manual now extant. That's this University of California publication.[63]

RITCHIE: I should like to see such a manual written by specialists and well illustrated, so that one could acquire a sound grasp of the various techniques. I would certainly not omit photography. I would use that as an introduction to field methods.

JOHNSON: Well, isn't it true that the proposed publication of what has gone on here in the last few days is a preliminary statement which eventually could be expanded and shaken down into something more useful?

WARD: I think we all want to see all types of evidence developed in the field. In listening to these talks I am impressed by the fact that almost everyone here is engaged in American archaeology, and that archaeology in America is largely taught in the departments of anthropology, so that all the people who dig have a pretty good idea of the types of evidence they should look for. When you turn to the Old World you find that the archaeologist does not come primarily from any department of anthropology. The Old World archaeologist may be a historian or a linguist or an Assyriologist, who has no idea of human culture as the anthropologist knows it, so he goes out and digs a site and leaves most of the evidence in the ground. Or he may be working for an art museum. No matter how much he tries to get evidence, in that case, he's not going to hunt for the remains of early cultivated plants from early sites when he's looking primarily for statues. Or he may want documents. Or he may also be a theologian. It seems to me that for all archaeologists who are working in the Old World (and that includes some Americans, although there are not as many as I wish there were), there is a great need for readily available standards of the kinds of evidence that any archaeological expedition should get.

[63]Heizer, ed., 1949.

Now in America we certainly need to increase our efficiency, but by and large almost everybody who goes on a dig here has had training and knows what ought to be done on a high-grade expedition. But in the Old World it's really a terrible situation. Old World archaeologists, when working on the most important sites, will often exhaust all of certain kinds of evidence and leave other equally important kinds of evidence completely unreported. Animal bones from early sites, where the beginning of domestication is a big problem, are usually left completely untouched. The bones are thrown away and frequently not even mentioned. I don't know that I have anything specific to propose to remedy this situation, but I wish that when, as here and now, we are examining the purposes and methods of archaeology, we should not forget the urgent need for establishing a minimum standard of efficiency for Old World excavations.

UNIDENTIFIED: Why would it not be possible to develop at least at one university a course or two devoted to a presentation, for both undergraduate and graduate students, of archaeological techniques and tools? Everyone knows, for example, the extreme importance of the camera in all fields of anthropology. It is perhaps most important in archaeology. Many students are not familiar with either photographic practice or theory. Little or no time is given in academic courses to even the most elementary instruction. In the field, either all photography is handled by an experienced man, or the student is given a camera and instructions to make a record of his work. Some universities have courses in photography; these should be recognized as cognate courses and students encouraged to take them. Wherever possible, field experience in photography should be provided.

The paper presented by Dr. Titterington is an example of one field of scientific knowledge applied to archaeology, which is rarely employed by the archaeologist, yet its value has been demonstrated many times. Some experimentation should be made to develop the applicability of X ray to an analysis of textiles, leather, and cloth.

Even such a comparatively common tool as the microscope is rarely, if ever, seen in an archaeological laboratory. Simple chemical tests for the identification of materials or the presence of important substances are not part of the students' training. The principles of spectroscopy, utilized by Root and Lundberg in their investigations, should be explained and their utility elaborated upon. Recently, the Federal Bureau of Investigation has been "fingerprinting" the surface soils of the United States by means of tracer elements. By this means, soil attached to a car impounded in northern Alabama may be proved to have recently been near Miami, Florida, for example. Would not this technique have value in the identification of foreign pottery?

These and many other applications of knowledge in other scientific fields should be called to the attention of students, as well as to the professional archaeologists. We should all be on the alert for such aids to cultural interpretations.

BREW: There's another aspect of this which can well be further emphasized. Learning what these techniques can do is very important, but we should teach students, also, what they will not do. I give a semester course in field methods. I am not at all satisfied with it, because I have had the same kind of experience as was outlined. I myself had no instruction whatever in any of these things; I came into American archaeology through classical archaeology and nothing about techniques was ever mentioned. In my field methods course where we deal with the dating techniques, dendrochronology, pollen analysis, geochronology, paleontology, C^{14}, and so forth, I think that I spend more time, actually, discussing the limitations of these techniques and evaluating them, than I do just explaining what they will do.

Students should have more of the type of presentation that we have had here today, where the techniques were presented accurately and honestly. When students get the knowledge of these things they usually have an entirely exaggerated opinion of what they can do, and they don't get a critical presentation of the techniques, such as was given today. It is important, particularly with regard to the dating techniques, and also with certain precision instruments, that students be taught just what these techniques and these instruments will not do, as well as what they will do.

GRIFFIN: I am convinced that all of us here are the Mooreheads and Hewitts of 1970, and I think that it is up to us to make certain that the students we are training have a broader schooling than was available to us. If we cannot improve the ability of our students to detect evidence which is valuable to them, which they can interpret as valuable cultural data, then we are simply failing in our obligations to our students, and that responsibility is, I think, one of the main points of this conference.

COOK: Mr. Chairman, may I make a remark to supplement some of the recent statements? It appears to me, if we are examining our premises, so to speak, that we should go back even a little further. The necessity for early acquaintanceship with points of view and methods has been pointed out, as well as the mere applications. But I should like to go back further and make a plea that those who interest themselves in archaeology and anthropology acquire some of the fundamental concepts of the sciences which otherwise would escape them, and in later years, even though they may not have the slightest mastery of technique, they may be able to understand the theory behind it and how it works in their own fields. Therefore, I would like to push the educational problem back from the graduate years to the freshman year. I won't say a word about secondary schools; I'll start with the university.

GRIFFIN: I think that's quite true; I think that there is a tendency among institutions, I know there is at Michigan, for dissatisfaction with the present undergraduate curriculum. In the introductory courses in the various fields, the material was presented with the assumption that the students were going on to specialize in chemistry, physics, botany, or zoology. But now there are being prepared nontechnical courses in physics, for instance, for students who are going into zoology, medicine, or other fields where they will need a knowledge of physics, but in which they are not treated as young Ph. D. candidates. Courses of this nature, if they can be developed, would be an asset to college and university curricula.

Participants

Lolita Binns	Wenner-Gren Foundation for Anthropological Research
Junius Bird	American Museum of Natural History
George W. Brainerd	Southwest Museum and University of California at Los Angeles
John O. Brew	Peabody Museum, Harvard University
Donald Collier	Chicago Natural History Museum
Sherburne F. Cook	University of California at Berkeley
Paul Fejos	Wenner-Gren Foundation for Anthropological Research
James A. Ford	American Museum of Natural History
Rutherford J. Gettens	Freer Art Gallery, Washington, D. C.
James B. Griffin	Museum of Anthropology, University of Michigan
Frederick Johnson	Robert S. Peabody Foundation for Archaeology
Samuel K. Lothrop	Peabody Museum, Harvard University
Hans Lundberg	Toronto, Canada
Frederick R. Matson	School of Mineral Industries, Pennsylvania State College
Frederick Orchard	Peabody Museum, Harvard University
Philip Phillips	Peabody Museum, Harvard University
Harry E. Pollock	Carnegie Institution of Washington
William A. Ritchie	New York State Museum

William C. Root   Bowdoin College

Irving Rouse   Department of Anthropology, Yale University

Albert C. Spaulding   Museum of Anthropology, University of Michigan

W. Duncan Strong   Department of Anthropology, Columbia University

Frederick P. Thieme   Department of Anthropology, University of Michigan

Paul F. Titterington   St. Louis, Missouri

Lauriston Ward   Peabody Museum, Harvard University

Waldo R. Wedel   United States National Museum

Selected Bibliography

American Antiquity
    1951 Radiocarbon Dating. Mem. Soc. Amer. Archaeol., No. 8.

Anonymous
    1928 Method of Preserving Mural Paintings in the Chapter House, Westminster Abbey. Mus. Journ., 28: 375-80.

Arnold, J. R., and W. F. Libby
    1949 Age Determination by Radiocarbon Content: Checks with Samples of Known Age. Science, 110, No. 2869: 678-80.

Barbour, Elizabeth P.
    1950 A Study of the Structure of Fresh and Fossil Human Bone by Means of the Electron Microscope. Amer. Journ. Phys. Anthropol., 8, No. 3: 315-29.

Beals, Ralph L., George W. Brainerd, and Watson Smith
    1945 Archaeological Studies in Northeast Arizona. Univ. Calif. Publ. Amer. Archaeol. and Ethnol., 44, No. 1:1-235

Bennett, Wendell C. (ed.)
    1948 A Reappraisal of Peruvian Archaeology. Mem. Soc. Amer. Archaeol., No. 4.

Bird, Junius
    1948 Preceramic Cultures in Chicama and Virú. In: A Reappraisal of Peruvian Archaeology, Wendell C. Bennett (ed.). Mem. Soc. Amer. Archaeol., No. 4: 21-28.

Bliss, Wesley L.
    1948 Preservation of the Kuaua Mural Paintings. Amer. Antiq., XIII, No. 3: 218-23.

Brainerd, George W.
    1951 The Place of Chronological Ordering in Archaeological Analysis. Amer. Antiq., XVI, No. 4: 301-13.

Brew, John O.
    1946 The Archaeology of Alkali Ridge, Southeastern Utah. Peabody Mus. Amer. Archaeol. and Ethnol., XXI: 1-345.

Bryan, Kirk
    1941 Correlation of the Deposits of Sandia Cave, New Mexico,

with the Glacial Chronology. Appendix to Evidence of Early Occupation in Sandia Cave, New Mexico, and Other Sites in the Sandia-Manzano Region, by Frank G. Hibben. Smithson. Misc. Coll., 99, No. 23.

Bryan, Kirk, and Louis L. Ray
1940 Geologic Antiquity of the Lindenmeier Site in Colorado. Smithson. Misc. Coll., 99, No. 2.

Carnot, Adolphe
1893 Recherches sur la composition générale et la teneur en fluor des os modernes et des os fossiles des différents âges. Ann. Mines, 3: 155-95 (9 Mem.).

Cook, S. F.
1951 The Fossilization of Human Bone: Calcium, Phosphate, and Carbonate. Univ. Calif. Publ. Amer. Archaeol. and Ethnol., Vol. 40, No. 6.

Coremans, Paul
1940 Peintures murales anciennes: procédés, altération, nettoyage et transfert. Bull. des Musées Royaux d'Art et d'Histoire (Bruxelles), No. 6: 133-316.

1941 Depose de peintures murales decouvertes en 1940 a Tournai et a Nivelles. Ibid., pp. 125-32.

de Terra, Hellmut, and T. T. Paterson
1939 Studies on the Ice Age in India and Associated Human Cultures. Carnegie Instit. Wash. Publ., No. 493.

Erdtman, Gunnar
1943 An Introduction to Pollen Analysis. Waltham, Mass.: Chronica Botanica Company.

Ford, James A.
1936 Analysis of Indian Village Site Collections from Louisiana and Mississippi. La. Dept. Conserv., Anthropol. Study, No. 2.

Ford, James A., and Gordon Willey
1949 Surface Survey of the Virú Valley, Peru. Anthropol. Paper Amer. Mus. Nat. Hist., Vol. 43, No. 1.

Forni, Ulisse
1866 Manuale del pittore restauratore. Florence: Successori Le Monnier Pp. 24-30.

BIBLIOGRAPHY

Foster, George M., assisted by Gabriel Ospina
   1948 Empire's Children, The People of Tzintzuntzan. Smithson. Instit., Instit. Soc. Anthropol. Publ., No. 6.

Gettens, Rutherford J.
   1935 Polymerized Vinyl Acetate and Related Compounds in the Restoration of Objects of Art. Tech. Studies in the Field of Fine Arts, 4: 15-27.

Greene, Francina S.
   n. d. Cleaning and Mounting Procedures for Wool Textiles. Workshop Notes, Paper No. 1, Textile Mus. Wash.

Greenman, Emerson F.
   1937 The Younge Site, An Archaeological Record from Michigan. Occ. Contrib. Mus. Anthropol. Univ. Mich., No. 6.

Guttman, Louis
   1944 A Basis for Scaling Qualitative Data. Amer. Sociol. Rev., 9: 139-50.

Heizer, Robert F. (ed.)
   1949 A Manual of Archaeological Field Methods. Millbrae, Calif.: National Press.

Hewes, Gordon B.
   1946 Early Man in California and the Tranquility Site. Amer. Antiq., XI, No. 4: 209-15.

Johnson, Frederick, and Hugh M. Raup
   1947 Grassy Island. Papers Peabody Found. Archaeol., Vol. 1, No. 2.

Johnson, Frederick, et al.
   1942 The Boylston Street Fishweir. Papers Peabody Found. Archaeol., Vol. 2.

   1949 The Boylston Street Fishweir. II. Ibid., Vol. 4, No. 1.

Kosolapoff, G. M.
   1951 Individualistic Statistical Approach. Science, 113: 129.

Kroeber, A. L.
   1948 Summary and Interpretations. In: A Reappraisal of Peruvian Archaeology, Wendell C. Bennett (ed.). Mem. Soc. Amer. Archaeol., No. 4: 113-21.

Kroeber, A. L., and W. Duncan Strong
   1924a The Uhle Collections from Chincha. Univ. Calif. Publ. Amer. Archaeol. and Ethnol., Vol. 21, No. 1.

1924b The Uhle Pottery Collections from Ica. Ibid., No. 3.

Krynine, P. D.
1939 Petrology of the Karewa Lake Beds. In: Studies of the Ice Age in India and Associated Human Cultures, by Hellmut de Terra and T. T. Paterson. Carnegie Instit. Wash. Publ., No. 493: 235-51.

Laudermilk, J. D.
1937 The Preservation of Textile Remains. Amer. Antiq., II, No. 4: 277-81.

Lavagnino, E.
1937 La conservation et la restauration des peintures murales. Mouseion, Nos. 39-40: 223-35.

Libby, W. F., E. C. Anderson, and J. R. Arnold
1949 Age Determination by Radiocarbon Content: World-Wide Assay of Natural Radiocarbon. Science, 109, No. 2828: 227-28.

Lothrop, Samuel K.
1942 Coclé, An Archaelogical Study of Central Panama. Peabody Mus. Archaeol. and Ethnol., Mem. No. 8.

Massoulard, Emile
1949 Prehistoire and protohistoire d'Egypte. Instit. d'Ethnol., Travaux et Mem., Vol. 53. Paris.

Matson, Frederick R., Jr.
1937 Pottery. Appendix to The Younge Site, An Archaeological Record from Michigan, by Emerson F. Greenman. Occ. Contrib. Mus. Anthropol. Univ. Mich., No. 6: 99-124.

Movius, Hallam L., Jr.
1949 Excavations at the Prehistoric Rock-Shelter of La Colombière. Archaeology, 2, No. 1: 22-30.

Oakley, Kenneth P.
1948 Fluorine and the Relative Dating of Bones. Advancement of Science, 4: 336-37.

1950 Relative Dating of the Piltdown Skull. Ibid., 6, No. 24.

1951 The Fluorine Dating Method. Yearbook of Phys. Anthropol., 1949. New York: The Viking Fund. Pp. 44-52.

Oakley, Kenneth P., and C. Randall Hoskins
1950 New Evidence on the Antiquity of Piltdown Man. Nature, 165: 379-88.

Oakley, Kenneth P., and M. F. Ashley Montagu
  1949 A Reconsideration of the Galley Hill Skeleton. Bull. Brit. Mus. Nat. Hist., Geol. ser., 1, No. 2: 25-48.

Raup, Hugh M.
  1942 Trends in the Development of Geographic Botany. Ann. Assoc. Amer. Geog., XXXII, No. 4.

Raup, Hugh M., and Frederick Johnson
  n. d. Archaeological, Botanical, and Geological Studies Along the Alaska Highway. In preparation.

Rinaldo, John
  1950 Analysis of Culture Change in the Ackmen-Lowry Area. Chicago Nat. Hist. Mus., Fieldiana, Anthropol., Vol. 36, No. 5.

Robinson, W. M.
  1951 A Method for Chronologically Ordering Archaeological Deposits. Amer. Antiq. XVI, No. 4: 293-301.

Rouse, Irving
  1939 Prehistory in Haiti, A Study in Method. Yale Univ. Publ. Anthropol., No. 21.

Shepard, Anna O.
  1936 The Technology of Pecos Pottery. In: The Pottery of Pecos, Papers of the Southwestern Expedition. New Haven: Yale Univ. Press. Vol. II, Pt. 2.

  1942 Rio Grande Glaze Paint Ware: A Study Illustrating the Place of Ceramic Technological Analysis in Archaeological Research. Contrib. Amer. Anthropol. and Hist. Vol. VII, No. 39, Carnegie Instit. Wash. Publ., No. 528.

  1948 The Symmetry of Abstract Design with Special Reference to Ceramic Decoration. Ibid., No. 574.

  n. d. Ceramics for the Archaeologist. In preparation.

Smith, Watson
  n. d. Prehistoric Kiva Mural Decorations of Awatovi and Kawaika-a. Peabody Mus. Amer. Archaeol. and Ethnol., Vol. 37. Chap. on Field Methods of Excavation, Preservation, and Reproduction. In preparation.

Spier, Leslie
  1917 An Outline for a Chronology of Zuni Ruins. Anthropol. Papers Amer. Mus. Nat. Hist., Vol. 18, Pt. 3.

Stewart, T. Dale
1951 Antiquity of Man in America Demonstrated by the Fluorine Test. Science, 113, No. 2936: 391-92.

Stopelaëre, A.
1942 Dégradations et restaurations des peintures murales Egyptiennes. ann. du Service des Antiq. de l'Egypte, 40: 941-50.

Stout, George L.
1935 Restauration d'un relief d'argile peint. Mouseion, Nos. 29-30: 105-11.

Stout, George L., and Rutherford J. Gettens
1932 Transport de fresques orientales sur de novaux supports. Mouseion, Nos. 17-18: 107-12.

Suardo, G. Secco
1918 Il restauratore dei Dipinti. Pt. 1, Chap. 3, 3d. ed. Milan.

Sylwan, Vivi
1941 Woolen Textiles of the Lou-lan People. Reports from Scientific Expedition to the North-western Provinces of China under the leadership of Dr. Sven Hedin (The Sino-Swedish Expedition). Publ. No. 15, Vol. VII, Archaeology 2. Stockholm.

1949 Investigation of Silk from Edsen-Gol and Lop-Nor. Ibid., Publ. No. 32, Vol. VII, Archaeology 6. Stockholm.

Tschopik, Harry, Jr.
1950 An Andean Ceramic Tradition in Historical Perspective. Amer. Antiq., XV, No. 3: 196-218.

White, W. C.
1937 Chinese Temple Fresco No. 1. Bull. Royal Ontario Mus. Archaeol., No. 12.

Whitford, A. C.
1941 Textile Fibers Used in Eastern Aboriginal North America. Anthropol. Papers Amer. Mus. Nat. Hist., Vol. 38, Pt. 1.

Willard, H. H., and O. B. Winter
1933 Volumetric Method for Determination of Fluorine. In: Industrial and Engineering Chemistry, analytical ed., 5: 7-10.

Willey, Gordon R.
 1945 Horizon Styles and Pottery Traditions in Peruvian Archaeology. Amer. Antiq., XI, No. 1: 49-56.

Zeuner, Frederick E.
 1946 Dating the Past, An Introduction to Geochronology. London: Methuen.

www.ingramcontent.com/pod-product-compliance
Lightning Source LLC
LaVergne TN
LVHW021231180326
833917LV00012B/388